THE BEAUTY IN
BEREAVEMENT

A PERSONAL STORY OF CHILD LOSS, GRIEF & MOVING FORWARD

First published by Ultimate World Publishing 2020
Copyright © 2020 Jasmin Hill

ISBN

Paperback: 978-1-922497-22-2
Ebook: 978-1-922497-23-9

Jasmin Hill has asserted her right under the Copyright, Designs and Patents Act 1988 to be identified as the author of this work. The information in this book is based on the author's experiences and opinions. The publisher specifically disclaims responsibility for any adverse consequences, which may result from use of the information contained herein. Permission to use information has been sought by the author. Any breaches will be rectified in further editions of the book.

All rights reserved. No part of this publication may be reproduced, stored in or introduced into a retrieval system, or transmitted in any form, or by any means (electronic, mechanical, photocopying, recording or otherwise) without the prior written permission of the author. Any person who does any unauthorised act in relation to this publication may be liable to criminal prosecution and civil claims for damages. Enquiries should be made through the publisher.

Cover design: Ultimate World Publishing
Layout and typesetting: Ultimate World Publishing
Editor: James Salmon

Ultimate World Publishing
Diamond Creek

Dedications

In memory of my sweet Bryson. Thank you for choosing me to be your mum, you are the brightest star in the sky my darling boy.

Jayme-Lee may your sweet little soul fly high, my beautiful nephew.

This book is dedicated to Lachlan, Hudson and Lincoln. Thank you for showing me what love is. You have all helped me heal in your own unique way.

Kelly Pritchard, thank you for your never-ending support. I always thought of myself as a burden, but you were quick to tell me that I was an absolute blessing. I love you.

The Beauty in Bereavement

Lisa Bartley, I am beyond grateful for your guidance and love throughout this horrible nightmare.

A special thank you to the amazing Chris Hester from Mantra Tattoo in Port Lincoln. You drew the perfect cover for my book, you are an absolute talent with an amazing heart.

A special mention to Sids & Kids NT, Still Aware, SANDS Australia and Bears of Hope. All four of these organisations have been such a huge help when Bryson died, and continue to support not only my family but many other families who are also suffering through their own grief.

Contents

Dedications	iii
Foreword	vii
CHAPTER 1: Where it all began	1
CHAPTER 2: I kissed a girl	9
CHAPTER 3: A roll of the dice	19
CHAPTER 4: The downward spiral	27
CHAPTER 5: The whirlwind of narcissism - part 1	39
CHAPTER 6: The whirlwind of narcissism – part 2	61
CHAPTER 7: Out of the friend zone	93
CHAPTER 8: There's no heartbeat	105
CHAPTER 9: Dear Bryson	129
CHAPTER 10: The tipping point	141
CHAPTER 11: A surprise wedding	161
CHAPTER 12: Irreplaceable	177
CHAPTER 13: Rainbows and postnatal	187
CHAPTER 14: My healing space	205
CHAPTER 15: Your final chapter	217

Foreword

"I'm so sorry for your loss." After my miscarriage, these words were not comforting. They implied that my child was gone, and sadness was the only emotion to be felt. I just couldn't accept that. Though part of my world for only a brief time, my baby impacted my heart greatly. So why would God give me the amazing gift of a child, only to take it back? With a legitimate question for God, there is really only one place I could look for His answer—in the Bible. In Jeremiah 1:5, I read:

> "Before I formed you in the womb, I knew you, before you were born, I set you apart."

So, not only does God intentionally form life in a mother's womb, but He also has a purpose and a plan for that life—not at birth—but clearly before? Oh, the peace and hope

The Beauty in Bereavement

For if God knew Jeremiah this way, He knows all He creates in the same way. My baby, your baby, every baby.

At that moment, I was ready to dedicate the rest of my life to finding my baby's purpose. I now had proof that he had one, I just hoped I would learn it on this side of eternity. In time, I began to think of the hundreds and thousands of devastated moms like me, who were hurting and could possibly begin to heal as I did, by learning this truth.

In 2013, nearly a year-to-date after my own miscarriage, I started a support group with the blessing of my church as its host. It was to be a place for hurting moms to gather weekly, seeking a space to share the love they felt for a baby that the world seemed to already forget.

The only thing is...dads showed up too! While this was not the reality of my own life, I was encouraged to see a circle full of couples amongst the tissue boxes ready to reveal a pain that nobody wanted to talk about. One of those couples was John and Tani Leeper.

They came to the group in a state of shock, fresh from their loss and desperate for a glimmer of hope. They wasted no time in challenging me, but each week I grew to appreciate their honesty and vulnerability. Tani was bold in her questioning to why this had happened to them. John, despite his own pain, just wanted to

Foreword

John came right out and asked, "When do we get your peace, when will that happen for all of us?"

Unfortunately, there is no formula or quick how-to-instructions. All I could do was share my story and invest myself in theirs. The amazing transformation that took place from there, you will have to read for yourself in this book.

As I write this, I realize our first meeting was over seven years ago. They have since become two of my closest friends, and I can't imagine my life without them. I am thankful to Baby Jake for bringing me his parents. It was his brief presence in this world that allowed our paths to cross. It breaks my heart that they weren't able to keep him here on earth. Although, I've heard it said: when you know where something is, it isn't really lost. We will see our babies again, but until then, God gave us each other.

This is their journey in healing and discovering their purpose...and it will inspire you.

Kim Preston
Angel Mom to Jeremiah
& Founder of In His Arms

CHAPTER 1

Where it all began

I was three years old when my family and I moved to Port Lincoln, South Australia. I still remember packing up my Sesame Street books into a plastic bag to bring in the car, so I could read them.

I moved into a nice little unit with my mum, her partner Geoff and my two older brothers, Christopher and Justin.

Mum and Dad separated when I was only a baby. Dad went on to marry a lady named Kay who already had children, Susan and Shalanda, and shortly after their marriage Kay and Dad welcomed a little baby girl into the world who they named Rikki-Lee.

The Beauty in Bereavement

I didn't get to see or speak to Dad a lot when I was little. We lived seven hours away from each other, Dad worked a lot and Mum didn't drive, so we would only see him and the family every once in a while.

Growing up in a house with my mum was difficult at times. Us kids were so young but would get up in the mornings and get ourselves ready for school whilst Mum slept. We would make our own sandwiches for lunch and I would always layer way too much vegemite on. I would sometimes forget to brush my hair or my teeth, but I tried my best. Our school was only around the corner from our house, so my brothers and I would walk to and from school every day.

By the time I was in Year Two, Mum and Geoff were accepted for a housing trust house. It was bigger and better but it was a half an hour walk from school.

Just after we all moved into our new house, Mum and Geoff separated, so it was just us kids and Mum.

Once I was in Year Four, I started to notice that Mum wasn't very maternal towards myself and my brothers. I don't recall being cuddled or kissed by her. We never did much as a family, and if Mum got up in the mornings in a bad mood, we would run to our rooms to hide out until she had a cup of tea and a cigarette. We never had a lot

Where it all began

from the salvos sometimes so Mum could feed us. To me, this was normal. I assumed every household was like ours.

Although Mum wasn't the most loving towards my brothers and I, I always noticed her helping my brother's friends if they were having trouble in their homes or needed somewhere to stay for a while. At the age of 11, my brother Christopher had his best friend Rocco move in with us permanently.

I knew Rocco, he would always visit Christopher prior to moving in with us. I trusted him just like he was one of my brothers, I would annoy him and my brothers by playing Hanson really loudly on my CD player, I would go out of my way to be a pain in the ass, because that's what little sisters did. I had 100% trust in Rocco, but that was all about to change.

One Friday night, Justin went to sleep at a friend's house. During the night I woke up after wetting the bed, so I got changed into some dry knickers and shorts then went straight into Justin's bed, which was a bunk bed. Christopher was on the top bunk and Rocco was on a mattress on the floor, right next to Justin's bed. I crept in, trying not to wake anyone up, got into Justin's bed, snuggled in and went back to sleep.

It must have been around 15 minutes later that I was

The Beauty in Bereavement

my leg. As I was wriggling my leg and starting to wake up properly, I figured out that it was someone's fingers making their way up my thigh. I was instantly frozen, I couldn't move or talk, I was simply frightened. I knew exactly who it was, although I had my back towards the person and my eyes shut as tight as could be. I knew it was Rocco. I could hear Christopher snoring so loud as all of this was happening, I was screaming out to him in my head, hoping he could somehow hear me, but he never woke up. As Rocco's fingers made their way into my underwear, my heart was beating out of my chest. I didn't want this to happen but I just couldn't move, it was like I was paralysed.

As I lay there being sexually abused by my brother's best friend, I was trying so hard to build up the courage to move away from Rocco. I kept thinking that if I didn't take action now, I could be raped, so I finally got the courage to roll over right up against the wall, as far away from Rocco as I could get, but he ended up moving onto the bed and abusing me again. I put up with it for around half an hour, then I eventually said go away, in a way that made it seem like I was saying it in my sleep, almost like I was sleep talking, which scared Rocco and he quickly went back onto the mattress where he laid silently for a few minutes.

I was up against the wall crying silent tears when I heard

Where it all began

cigarette, came back into the bedroom and smoked the cigarette in his bed. I stayed in the exact same spot until the next morning, then as soon as my brother woke up and got out of bed, I got out and walked with him. I didn't even look to see if Rocco was asleep or not, I went straight into the shower where I cried my 11-year-old heart out.

I wasn't sure how to tell my mum, I was too ashamed to say anything. My friend Shelby from school came over to visit me that morning, I was sitting on the couch not really talking to her, so she knew something was wrong. I told Shelby everything, she was so supportive and got me to tell Mum. I sat on Mum's bed and told her everything. Mum asked me a couple of questions about what had happened then told me to leave it with her.

I left her room and saw Rocco sitting in the kitchen with my brother, and although he couldn't look me in the eye, he was still laughing and messing around with my brother as if nothing had happened. Mum came out of her bedroom, walked straight past the boys in the kitchen and continued on with her morning cleaning, as if I hadn't just told her I was sexually abused the night before. I was in complete shock and was very confused. I thought that she would have yelled at Rocco or kicked him out, but she didn't say one word to him. Shelby ended up going home and I went into my bedroom, shut my door and stayed there all day. Mum would pop her head in to see

The Beauty in Bereavement

Mum never ended up saying anything to Rocco that day, or any other day. She allowed Rocco to remain under our roof. A few months went by and I noticed Rocco trying to build my trust with him again, he would tell me jokes or pick me up over his shoulder and run as fast as he could. Although I didn't trust him completely, I thought maybe I needed to give him a second chance because he wasn't leaving our house any time soon, so everything went back to normal around home. I even became comfortable enough to sleep in the lounge room on Friday nights so I could watch Rage the next morning.

One particular Friday night, I dragged my mattress from my bedroom into the lounge room. I decided I would try to stay up as late as I could watching movies. I remember drifting off with the TV still turned on. Just as I was falling asleep and starting to dream, I felt those same fingers touching my legs but this time I wasn't afraid, I jumped up and yelled at the top of my lungs, 'DON'T YOU DARE TOUCH ME!' Rocco quickly ran back into his bedroom as I ran to Mum's bedroom door, swung it open, ran over to her and said, 'Mum he's doing it again'. I didn't have to say anything else, Mum knew exactly what and who I meant. I stayed in her room as she went into the boys' bedroom to check on Rocco.

She returned to tell me that he was in his bed pretending to be asleep. I sat on the ground crying – Mum hadn't said

Where it all began

about what was happening to me and why my own mother wasn't calling the police or yelling at this monster.

I spent the next couple of weeks sitting in my bedroom sobbing, pulling my hair out and blaming myself for everything that had happened. I would sleep with Mum every night, I barely showed my face in my own home. I think Mum got the hint that I was feeling very uncomfortable and finally asked Rocco to move out. When Rocco asked why he was being kicked out, Mum answered with, 'I think you know why'. That was it, nothing else was said to Rocco, he got to move out of my home, knowing he had gotten away with sexually abusing me. Once he had gone, Mum never really brought the abuse up again. She never asked if I was ok, or if I wanted to call the police. Rocco was gone and I was made to move on all alone.

I struggled through the next four years of my life. I often used sarcasm as a defence mechanism with pretty much everything, it was the only way I coped with everything on my own. Just after I turned 15, I was with a bunch of school friends, one of them handed me a bottle of Vodka and told me to have a sip, I agreed and after that first taste, I was hooked. I very quickly learned that the alcohol was numbing my mind and heart – I enjoyed it a lot.

It didn't take long for me to start drinking on a daily

supermarket and would get wasted as soon as I finished my shift.

The numbness of the alcohol didn't last as long as I would have hoped. It just ended up making me angry, mainly at myself for not being strong enough to stop Rocco from ever touching me.

I would be out at my friend's house drinking and would think to myself, 'Well if this monster can abuse me without my permission, I can give myself permission to abuse my body whenever I feel like it'. That was when I decided to start having sex. I was never sober when I had sex, I had to be completely and utterly obliviated to do it. I never enjoyed sex or abusing my body, but a piece of me also thought that abusing my body was normal.

I was going to keep drinking and being out of control until it killed me and I was ok with that.

CHAPTER 2

I kissed a girl

Just after I turned 17, I was driving around the streets of Port Lincoln with my childhood friend, Shelby. I had my box of wine, Shelby had the music blaring and we were talking shit, just like all 17-year-olds do. I remember driving past a particular house and seeing a family outside. I spotted a girl who was dressed in boys clothing, I asked Shelby if she knew the family, and she said she knew of the tomboy, and that her name was Anna. I mentioned that Anna was kind of cute, Shelby laughed and said, *'I have dibs on Anna'*, which was funny because neither Shelby or I were lesbians. I had found myself looking at other girls before and never questioned my sexuality because of it, but Anna grabbed my attention

The Beauty in Bereavement

A few days later whilst sitting down the main street with a couple of friends, I saw a beautiful blonde girl approaching us. It turns out it was Anna's sister, Jean. She was cousins with one of my friends I was sitting with. We got to talking and she ended up inviting me over to her house. Her words were, *'Oi ya mole, you should come over my house'* – I had a good laugh about that. Jean was definitely my type of person, so I told her I would come over on the weekend with some friends.

Saturday night came around and I stuck to my word. I went to visit Jean and met her mum, dad, little brother and her sister, Anna.

I was pretty drunk by the time I arrived but I had a good conversation with Anna's mum. Her name was Vicky, she had burgundy coloured hair, lovely green eyes, and was very quick to tell us that she had rules for her kids at home. Vicky's kids weren't allowed to go out to parties, or cruise around late at night like I was. They had to wait until they were 18. Jean was only 15 at the time, so she had a few years to go until she was allowed to party and have fun but Anna was turning 18 in three weeks.

Anna was fairly quiet the night that we first met, I actually kept forgetting she was there. I loved hearing Vicky's stories of how protective she was of her kids, and seeing the collection of swords she had in her house. I kept thinking, *'I wish my mum*

I kissed a girl

After spending a couple of hours chatting to my new friends I said goodbye, but I promised Jean that I would come back to see them all again.

The next day, I caught up with Jean and Anna. We lounged around watching movies all day and I slowly got to know Anna a bit more. Anna worked at a fish factory, she loved cars and hated anything girly.

As the days went by, Anna and I started to spend every day together and if I wasn't at her house, we were on the phone to each other. We were inseparable.

The day Anna turned 18, she bought herself a carton of bourbon, said goodbye to her mum and we spent the whole afternoon and evening being driven around by one of our friends.

Once the alcohol was gone, we decided it was time to sleep, but Anna didn't want to go home, she wanted to spend the night away from there and sleep at her cousin's. Anna called her cousin, Cody, to ask if we could stay over. Cody was fine with it, so we headed over to his place.

When we got there, Cody had made up the bed in the spare room for us to sleep on. We said goodnight to Cody, shut the door and got into bed. We lay in bed, face to face, pretty much as close as you could get without touching kiss Anna so bad, but I wasn't sure if she would react very well to it. I had never asked Anna if she was a lesbian, and she had never told me she was a lesbian, so I was scared that this kiss would get me a slap in the face. I thought it was best if I didn't go ahead with the kiss and just went to sleep, but just as I shut my eyes, I felt Anna's lips kiss mine. She quickly rolled over – she was feeling the same way as I was, unsure how I would react as well. I rolled her back over towards me and kissed her again, and after we got our first kiss out of the way, we snuggled up together and went to sleep.

The next morning, we woke up, had a bit of a giggle about the night before and that was it, it wasn't awkward at all. Vicky ended up coming over to Cody's to pick Anna and I up. She dropped me home so that they could have some family time with Anna. It didn't stop us from texting each other for the rest of the day and calling each other that night. I felt like I was developing some sort of feelings for Anna, I felt like it may have been love, but I wasn't entirely sure what love felt like. As the days went on, the bond between Anna and I grew stronger and stronger, until finally, Anna asked me to be her girlfriend. I said, 'Hell yeah'.

Anna and I had decided to keep our relationship from as many people as possible. She was unsure how her mum would react, so we only told Shelby. Anna and I would reminded us of each other whilst secretly holding hands. We enjoyed keeping our relationship hidden but we knew eventually we would have to tell our loved ones, so we decided to tell my mum first. I was technically still living at Mum's although I was never there. Mum had met Anna already and she wasn't at all shocked when I told her we were dating. Although Mum wasn't the most maternal person on the planet, she still accepted me for who I was and said, *'As long as you are both happy, then that's all that matters'*. Mum had also mentioned how I wasn't drinking as much since being in Anna's life and she was right. I wasn't binge drinking anymore – I just didn't feel the need to do it.

Anna and I had decided to spend more time at my place now that my mum knew about our relationship, until one afternoon when Anna and I were taking a shower together, we heard a knock on the bathroom door. Before I could ask who was there, Jean walked in. Anna and I were standing there, in shock. Jean made some joke about us showering together, told us she would meet us in the lounge room and walked out. Anna and I got straight out of the shower, quickly got dressed and went to see Jean. Anna was so nervous to tell Jean that we were showering together because we were a couple but as soon as she said those words, Jean looked Anna dead in the eye and said, *'I'm not fucking stupid, I know you're a lesbian'*. I couldn't help but laugh. Jean was completely unfazed by the whole thing, take news as bad as what she thought. Anna decided it was time to tell her mum that she was gay.

Anna went home to ask if I could sleep over at their house for the night. Vicky said, *'Of course, you don't even have to ask that question'*. Anna went on to ask if I could sleep in Anna's bed with her. Vicky looked at Anna with a strange look on her face and said, *'I guess so, but why?'* and that's when Anna blurted out, *'Because I'm gay and Jasmin's my girlfriend'*. Vicky smiled with tears filling up her eyes, gave Anna a big cuddle and said, *'You know I will always support your decisions, and I love you'*.

After Vicky knew, Anna told the rest of her family. Most people seemed to take the news well, but there were a few of Anna's relatives who I didn't really associate with that didn't take the news so well and decided to cut Anna out of their lives. That hurt Anna a little bit but she soon realised it wasn't worth even worrying about. Her happiness was all that mattered.

I ended up moving in with Anna once everyone knew about our relationship. I liked it at Anna's house. Although Anna and her siblings argued a lot, they loved and supported each other.

The first year of our relationship was really great, but I was noticing myself actually falling in love with Anna, and

I kissed a girl

time I felt like my heart belonged to her. I wasn't sure why this kept happening and it would just make me so angry. I would tell Anna I loved her all the time, but I couldn't quite show love the way she showed love.

I wasn't the type to hug and kiss all the time, but Anna was and it annoyed me if she wanted too much affection. Even though I struggled with my emotions and I could clearly see it was hurting Anna, Anna proposed to me whilst we were away for the weekend visiting my family. I said *'Yes'*.

Legally we couldn't get married in Australia so we weren't going to plan a wedding anytime soon, but it felt nice to have someone love me enough to want to marry me.

Not long after Anna proposed, we started to get into some pretty intense arguments. When we argued, I would always become so angry that I would yell, scream, hit, bite, do anything I could to release my anger. Sometimes Anna would fight back and hit me, but most of the time she just let me go. I would always end up apologising and Anna would always end up forgiving me. She had a big heart and some serious patience for me.

After our two-year anniversary, I realised I was really unhappy. I loved Anna dearly, but I knew it was a love that I would have for a best friend, not a partner. I started to

The Beauty in Bereavement

with both males and females. I didn't know how to tell Anna that I didn't love her the way she loved me. I felt gutless, so Anna and I remained together as a couple but I would live my life as if I was single. Anna knew about some of the stuff I would get up to – Port Lincoln is a small town and people talked – but she stood by me.

Although I was the one demolishing our relationship, I was always trying to fix it too. We would go away to Alice Springs for a few months for work, I would behave, we would miss home, so we would move back. As soon as I was back home, I would go out and continue to cheat on Anna.

After almost five years of fun for me and torture for Anna, we decided we would move to Darwin. My mum had moved to Darwin with her new partner, Mike, so we thought we would give our relationship one last try and head off to the tropics.

As soon as we arrived on the plane and walked out of the airport into the mugginess of the wet season, I knew I was home.

Mum allowed Anna and I to live with her and Mike, and I managed to score myself a job at the local casino as a slots attendant. The job wouldn't start for another couple of weeks so I lapped up the Darwin heat, and swam in was to be in Darwin. She seemed miserable and instead of asking her if she was ok, I snapped at her, telling her to stop being a miserable bitch, which led to a huge argument between the both of us, the biggest one we had ever had. We were screaming, I was throwing stuff at her, she was calling me names. It was just unhealthy and so toxic. Eventually Anna had enough of my shit and she finally left me.

I don't think I could have ever had the strength to leave Anna for good, so to watch her walk out the door made me realise that she was a lot stronger than I was.

She dropped by a couple of weeks after we separated to grab some of her stuff, we said goodbye, she got in the car and drove off.

Although Anna was staying in Darwin, I felt like she had left the country. I was going to miss her so much; I had completely fucked up five years of her life for my own selfishness.

I was glad she had gone to start a new chapter of her life. I was so angry at myself for hurting her the way I had, for taking out all of my anger on her and for not being the partner she deserved.

Chapter 3

A roll of the dice

Although I was feeling a little lost without Anna, I was excited to finally be starting my new job at the casino. I hadn't worked in a long time, and I was feeling really anxious about learning the ropes.

Luckily I had a lovely lady named Georgia who trained me. She was an older lady and had been working in slots for many years, so she gave me the rundown on the other staff members. Who to avoid, who was nice, and it was really nice to get a head start on who everyone was before meeting them all. At the end of my shift, I went into the office to fill out some paperwork when I saw a girl sitting on the work desk waiting to start her shift. She seemed

The Beauty in Bereavement

got to talking, and it turned out she was actually really lovely, her name was Simone and she was going to be training me the following day.

My next shift rolled around and I walked into the office at work, and there was Simone waiting patiently for me to arrive. As soon as our shift started, Simone and I started chatting about our lives, and it turned out we had a lot in common. We both had a love for chocolate, we both had super pale skin, we loved the same TV shows and we both had a wicked sense of humour. Simone was dating another slots attendant by the name of Cody – she introduced me to him once he started his shift. He was also quiet, didn't say a lot, and if he did talk, it was sarcasm. I didn't really see what Simone saw in him, but she was happy and that was all that mattered.

Over the next few days, Simone continued to train me. We had received a job over the other side of the casino, right near the bar, and as we approached the job I just happened to look over at the bar and there stood a young man. He had hair just past his ears, piercings in his lip and one beautiful set of blue eyes. As soon as I saw him, I grabbed Simone's arm and said, *'Oh my god, who is that?'* then I blurted out, *'I'm going to marry him one day'*. Simone and I both had a giggle about what I had just said, but something inside my heart and mind was saying, *'That man is going to be a huge part of your life one*

A roll of the dice

something like that, but there was something so attractive about this man. Simone asked me to collect some empty drink glasses from around the pokie machines and take them over to the bar. I collected a handful and made my way over to the bar. I had all intentions on smiling at the handsome young man that I had literally just told Simone I was going to marry, but as soon as he locked eyes with me, I dumped the empty glasses on the bar and ran off like an embarrassed school girl. I had no idea what was wrong with me, I could easily talk to anyone, I would talk to a tree if it spoke back to me, so I wasn't too sure what the hell just happened.

After that, I never wanted to go near the bar at all, but I had to do my job and return empty glasses. The young man would smile at me and say 'Hi' and I would talk some sort of gibberish under my breath with an awkward smile on my face, turn around and walk away as fast as I could. I'm pretty certain that the young man who I was crushing on knew that maybe I liked him, or that I had a speech problem. I was just thankful I had the day off the next day, so I didn't have to embarrass myself for an entire 24 hours.

It was my birthday on my day off. I was turning 23, and I had invited everyone in the slots department out for drinks. Though I wasn't really close with them all, I thought I would be nice and just invite everyone.

The Beauty in Bereavement

I knew Simone was coming but I assumed no one else would, so I was shocked to see so many people rock up and want to party with me. I hadn't been drunk in a long time but I was happy to let my hair down and have a good time. Simone and I got so drunk, we were doing shots at the bar, dancing and having the best time. I started to realise that Simone wasn't as shy as I thought, she was actually a lot of fun and although we had only known each other for a short time, I classed her as a close friend already.

Once the celebrations were over and it was time to go back to work, I decided to take a leap of faith and speak to the young man who had me tongue-tied. I wanted to reassure him that I could in fact speak, I was just a bit shy, which was obviously a load of crap, but how else could I explain my behaviour? As I went up to the staff canteen, I spotted the mystery man sitting outside on his break. I took a deep breath, walked outside and sat right next to him. I saw his name badge, it said 'Lachie' – finally the man had a name. I asked Lachie how his day was going and if it was busy, all the normal work chit chat. We only got to speak for five minutes then we both had to go to work, but as Lachie walked off he said *'Talk to you later'* with the cheekiest smile on his face.

There was something about the way he smiled at me and the way his eyes looked into mine.

A roll of the dice

I had a feeling that maybe Lachie liked me the same way that I liked him, which is why I was shocked when a work mate of mine had told me that Lachie had a girlfriend. I was never the one to dwell on anything or allow my feelings to get hurt, so I just sucked up the disappointment and got on with my life.

I was excited that my older brother, Christopher, was in Darwin visiting Mum, Mike and myself. I organised a night out on the town with him, my work mate, Mel, and her husband. We started off at a nice quiet bar, where Mel and I chatted and got to know each other more. Mel was a lot like me, she had previously been in a same-sex relationship and she loved a drink or two. The more drinks Mel and I had, the more we wanted to go to a club and dance. Mel's husband had work in the morning so he caught a taxi home, Christopher tagged along with us to the club where the drinks really started to flow and my bank account started to drain. I remember standing at an ATM inside the club, withdrawing $1000 and handing it out like it was candy.

Shit got really foggy around 3am, I was an absolute mess. I remember being outside the club, lying in the gutter, yelling out to Christopher and Mel, who I had lost throughout the night. I remember a man asking if I was ok, he asked me for my address, wrote it down on a piece of paper and handed it to a police officer who was standing nearby. The man was

was busy handling other drunk people that were causing a scene outside the club. The man ended up helping me out of the gutter, holding me up and walking me back to his hotel. I don't remember the whole walk home, but I do remember thanking the man for looking after me.

I remember barely standing up in a shower and climbing into bed with the man and that was it.

The next morning, I was woken up by my phone ringing over and over. As my eyes slowly started to open, I saw a complete stranger standing on the other side of the bed, texting someone on his phone. I soon realised I was butt naked which probably meant we had sex. As I sat up, I asked the man his name, he told me it was Adrian.

'I probably should have asked that before we slept together,' I joked.

Adrian laughed. *'Yeah that probably would have made things less awkward today,'* he replied.

As I was trying to put the pieces of the puzzle together from the night before, I checked my phone. 23 missed calls from my mother and ten missed calls from my brother. I quickly called my mum and let her know I was ok and that I had stayed at a friends the night before. There was no way I was going to tell her I was in a random hotel room

A roll of the dice

Adrian offered to drop me home on his way to work, and I knew I couldn't afford to get a taxi after draining my bank account, so I took him up on the offer. On the way to my house, I asked Adrian if he was from Darwin. Turns out he was in town briefly for work – he was actually from Queensland.

Once we were outside my house, I apologised for the night before. I was pretty ashamed of myself.

'It's fine, I enjoyed looking after you,' Adrian replied. I shut the car door, waved goodbye and Adrian drove off.

I was relieved to be home safely, and glad that no one knew about my drunken one-night stand.

I was taking this secret to the grave – at least that's what I thought anyway.

Chapter 4

The downward spiral

It was May of 2009, which meant one thing...PINK CONCERT! I was always a lover of music, and Pink was hands down my favourite female singer. A few days before I flew to Adelaide for the concert, I got my period. It was really early, which never happened, but it was also really light and painless, and only lasted around two days. I never found it odd, I was actually happy and assumed my period would most probably be that way from now on.

The day I landed in Adelaide was the day of the concert, and as soon as Pink hit the stage, my jaw hit the floor. She performed her acrobatic style show and sung in perfect tune the entire time. I was really emotional at the concert for some reason, I would have tears building up when she would sing certain songs. I thought it must have been the electricity from Pink and from the crowd.

I spent three days in Adelaide, complaining about the cold weather the entire time, so I was glad when I arrived back in Darwin to a beautiful dry season. The day I got back I noticed my clothes were getting a little big for me, I was losing weight, and I was pretty happy with that as I had been wanting to lose a few kilos for a while. Over the next couple of weeks, I noticed my boobs were really sore, and found myself becoming really hungry all the time. I would eat but would keep losing weight. Someone from work suggested I could be pregnant, but I laughed and said, *'You have to have sex to fall pregnant'*. As those words came out of my mouth, Adrian popped into my head. I wasn't even sure if we used protection, but I had my period after we slept together, so I couldn't possibly be pregnant.

That night I went into the chemist and got a pregnancy test just to put my mind at ease. I was confused looking at all of the tests, I had no idea what to buy. I think the lady behind the counter could see how confused I was because she ended up asking me if I needed a hand choosing a test. I asked for a cheap test, because in my eyes I was wasting my time and money on the damn thing.

I paid for my $6 test, went home, opened up the box and peed on the test, just like the instructions said. I put the test on top of the toilet, near the flush button, looked at myself in the bathroom mirror and started to lecture myself. *'Jasmin, you are too young for a baby, you aren't ready for this,'* I told myself as I waited for three minutes to pass by. I didn't even get to a minute when I glanced over at the test and almost died from shock when I saw that it was a big fat positive. I grabbed the test and ran out to Mum yelling, *'Mum, look at this'*. Mum had no idea what the test was, she had never taken a pregnancy test in her life. When I told her it was a positive pregnancy test and it was mine, she was just as shocked as I was.

I had to tell her about my one-night stand with Adrian for her to find out who the father was.

I've had some awkward times in my life, and that conversation was top three of the most awkward. Mum didn't judge me though; she was just happy she was going to be a nana.

I called my dad to tell him the news. Dad was happy for me but worried about me being a single mum. I was afraid to raise this child alone, but it's not like I could just call Adrian and tell him he was going to be a father. I didn't even know if that was his real name, I wouldn't even know where to begin to track him down. I was anti-abortion so that wasn't even an option in my eyes, so I decided to raise the baby on my own, with the help of Mum. After a visit to the doctor and a blood test, I found out that I was five weeks pregnant and the period I thought I had was implantation bleeding.

It didn't take long for the morning sickness to take over. I started off feeling dizzy and barely being able to stand up at work, to being bedridden at home. I would vomit all day and all night, I stopped eating, I was barely drinking and was making frequent visits to the hospital to rehydrate my body.

If I wasn't at the doctor or the hospital, I was completely bedridden at home. I had a doctor visit to attend when I was ten weeks along, and as soon as I stepped into the doctor's office, the doctor looked at me and told me to get on the scale to weigh myself. I got on and looked at the numbers that popped up – I was 39 kilograms. I was 65 kilograms just before I fell pregnant. The doctor sent me straight to accident and emergency. I was admitted straight away, with a drip put into my arm.

Mum came to the hospital and dropped me off a sandwich. I was able to have three bites. I was so proud of myself; I hadn't eaten properly in weeks so those three bites were an achievement for me.

The day after I was admitted to hospital, I was sent for an ultrasound to check on the baby. The sonographer put the cold gel on my tummy, as I lay on the bed staring at the screen, waiting to see the little baby who was making me so sick. As soon as I saw the baby, my heart melted, I kept saying how cute it was. The sonographer mentioned that the baby looked very healthy but was sucking every last nutrient out of me. It was so beautiful seeing my baby for the first time, this was a human life that I had created and couldn't wait to hold.

The sonographer said she would print off some pictures of the ultrasound, then I could head back to the ward I was staying on. I don't know what happened to the pictures but I was wheeled straight back to my ward without them, and I never ended up receiving them.

I spent three days in hospital. The doctors weren't too sure as to why I was so sick and losing weight so rapidly. One of the doctors who assessed me suggested I may have to think about a termination due to my illness being so severe, and as much as I wanted to say he was full of shit, I knew he made a great point. I was deteriorating and although the baby was fine, I was far from being ok.

I ended up being discharged and went straight home, but as soon as I walked through my front door, I began to spew again. I was bedridden and couldn't eat or drink again. Mum came home from work and popped her head through my bedroom door to check on me. I asked her to come in so I could talk to her.

'I can't carry this baby anymore,' I said to Mum. Mum was very understanding, she could see what the pregnancy

was doing to me, and she said whatever decision I made, it would be the right one. After thinking about making the worst decision I could ever make, I made the dreaded phone call to organise a termination. After having a long talk over the phone and even dragging myself into my doctor, my appointment to have my termination was scheduled.

I had to wait seven more days before I could have the termination, which in my eyes, meant seven more days of pure torture. The night before the termination, I had a dream that I was all of a sudden cured and felt amazing. I was yelling out, *'I'm better, I don't have to kill my baby now'*. It felt awful to wake up and find out that I was still sick. I dragged myself from my bed, got into the shower, stood under the water and spewed all over the floor. I hated that my pregnancy had come to this. I hated that I had let my baby down. I hated myself so much but I knew what was right and the termination was the right decision.

When I arrived at the hospital a lovely nurse called me into a room and began telling me what to expect from the STOP.

'What's a STOP?' I asked, very confused. The nurse told me that they didn't use the word abortion or termination, they used STOP, instead. I don't know why, but when she said that, I got really pissed off. I was told to get undressed, put on a hospital gown, sit down and wait for my name

The downward spiral

to be called by the surgeon who was performing my termination.

I sat with my head down the entire time. I didn't want to look at anyone, I kept thinking about my baby, I always thought it would be a boy. I had the name 'Callum' picked out if it was.

My name was called, and I slowly got up and made my way to a room where I met the surgeon. He was so lovely and understanding towards me, I told him I didn't want to do it and could I leave if I wanted to. He said yes but I never left. I got onto the bed, lay down, watched a mask coming towards my face, closed my eyes tight, and began to say sorry to my baby inside my head. It felt like I was out for five minutes when I felt someone gently touching my arm and calling out to me.

It was over. I had terminated my baby. I was devastated inside my heart but I kept myself looking strong on the outside. I went into recovery and sat on a recliner, where I smashed down a whole sandwich. My body was instantly back to normal, I had an appetite again. I couldn't believe it. I was discharged a short time after I ate the sandwich, and as Mum's partner, Mike, drove me out of the hospital car park I noticed a group of people standing on a patch of grass with signs and a table set up. I looked over to read their signs – they were people protesting against abortions. I took one look at those people and thought, *'If only you knew what I just did'*.

I spent the next few days eating all of the food I wanted to eat while I was pregnant. I had fairy floss, cheeseburgers, chocolate – you name it, I probably ate it.

I was bleeding a lot after the surgery, and I felt like the bleeding wasn't slowing down either. I went to the toilet to check on my bleeding and noticed a massive clot. I freaked out and showed Mum, she got Mike and took me straight to Accident and Emergency. On the way there I felt more and more clots coming out of me, I felt drained and I was white as a ghost.

When we arrived, Mum explained my situation to the nurse behind the counter. She got me a wheelchair and wheeled me straight into the emergency room, where I was met by a team of doctors. I had morphine pumped into me and was hooked up to a heart monitor. I was told I was haemorrhaging. I started to panic. I assumed I was going to die, then the morphine kicked in and I started to laugh at everything. Mum and Mike were having a good giggle at me rolling around the bed in extreme pain, but laughing from being off my face on drugs.

After everything settled and I was admitted into hospital, a doctor told me that the termination I had didn't go to plan, and not everything was cleaned out properly. *'So I have bits of my dead baby inside me,'* I said, bluntly. The doctor tried sugar-coating the situation but I wasn't about sugar-coating. I saw the situation for what it was, a complete fucking mess.

The downward spiral

I was pumped full of antibiotics for almost a week then given the all clear to go home.

I was thankful to recover and not bleed to death, but I was so angry at the surgeon for not doing his job properly and almost killing me.

Mum and Mike picked me up from the hospital and began to drive me home. Mum was having a bitch about my brother, Justin, who was visiting at the time and the fact he was drinking all the coke in the fridge. I ended up saying *'I've just got out of hospital and don't want to hear this shit'*.

Mum snapped back and said, *'You think you've got it rough, I can guarantee my life was worse when I was younger'*. I just shut my mouth; I was too tired to argue with anyone about anything.

Once I was home, I locked myself in my room for almost two weeks straight. I didn't come out unless I needed food or water. No one checked on me either. I felt like the biggest piece of shit. I had aborted my child, haemorrhaged and all of a sudden Mum couldn't care less that I went through hell.

A month after I haemorrhaged, Mum and I started to talk again, but nothing about my termination was mentioned. I wasn't asked if I was ok, which didn't surprise me at all, but for some reason it still hurt me.

I was due to go back to work now that I was fully recovered, and I couldn't wait to see Simone. I had pushed everyone away the past few weeks so it felt great knowing I was going to see her and my other work mates.

My first day back, I went into the changerooms to put my uniform on and my pants fell straight off of me. I had to race to the uniform shop to grab a size 8 pants and top. I couldn't believe how thin I was. Although I had put on a little bit of weight, I was still so thin. I walked into work, where I was greeted lovingly by everyone. I had told everyone, except for my close friends, that I had miscarried. I was too ashamed to admit I had a termination. I think it felt like I had miscarried as well, because I wanted the baby so badly and never wanted the termination.

Simone pulled me aside at work and apologised for not being there for me during my pregnancy.

'Don't be silly, you weren't to know how bad it had got for me,' I said.

'I could have just sat with you while you were sick,' she replied.

I felt so loved by Simone. I gave her a big cuddle and thanked her for being a great best friend. Although she wasn't around when I was sick, at least I knew she loved me. I saw Lachie just as I finished my first shift back, it

The downward spiral

was great to see him. He gave me a big wave and said hello, I waved back with a goofy smile on my face, like I always did when I saw him.

Once I got back into the swing of things at work, I also got back into my drinking. I was going to the pub as much as I could, and I would drink until I couldn't drink anymore. I wasn't coping with the termination, so I chose to go back to old habits and drink my feelings away. I was going into work drunk or hungover all the time. I was hitting rock bottom fast, but I was secretly enjoying it. This was the way I coped with trauma or pain, so I didn't see the issue with my binge drinking at the time.

One afternoon, I came into work really hungover. I started to approach the cashier to collect my money for my shift when I saw Lachie walking towards me. He looked so happy. I asked why he was so happy, he grabbed me, did a little happy dance with me, dipped me, told me it was his last shift because he was moving back to South Australia and just like that, he was gone.

I was left in shock. He skipped off so fast that I didn't even get to say a proper goodbye.

I stood near the cashier thinking, 'Well, that's that. I won't ever see him again.'

Goodbye Lachie, I will miss you.

Chapter 5

The whirlwind of narcissism - part 1

I had been at the casino for quite some time now. I loved my job a lot but I felt like something was missing in my life. One night I was chatting to my sister, Rikki-Lee – Rikki had just had a baby and was feeling quite lonely and sad, which made me feel sad for her. I made a quick decision to leave Darwin and head for Adelaide.

I went over to Simone's house to say goodbye. She ended up crying, I was shocked when I saw the tears rolling down her face. As much as I hated to see Simone cry, it felt good knowing that someone loved and cared for me enough to miss me like Simone was going to. I didn't shed any tears. I always had that guard up with my emotions, I could very quickly shut them off when I felt I needed to. I was just as sad as Simone, but I just couldn't bring myself to show her the same emotions as she was showing me.

Once we said our goodbyes, I left for Adelaide. I didn't tell work I was leaving, I just left.

As soon as I got to Adelaide, I went straight to my dad's house. Dad was working away but my stepmum, Rikki-Lee and her daughter, Paityn, were all there. It was great meeting my niece for the first time, she was such a little princess with the prettiest blue eyes. As I held Paityn for the first time, I found myself thinking about my pregnancy and whether our babies would have looked similar.

Later that evening, my stepsister Shalanda popped over to say hello. I hadn't seen Shalanda in years, so once we started chatting, we didn't stop. The subject of my termination came up – I knew my sisters would never judge me for my decision and I felt comfortable sharing my story to them. After I shared my story, Shalanda started to share her story. Turns out, back in 2004, Shalanda had a baby boy who was stillborn, who she named Jayme-Lee. I always knew my sister had a baby that had died, but I never knew it was stillbirth. I didn't really even know what the word meant. Shalanda spoke about the lead up to Jayme-Lee's death, the ultrasound that confirmed his death, the birth of Jayme-Lee and his funeral. Rikki,

The whirlwind of narcissism - part 1

Shalanda and myself all sat on the couch bawling our eyes out. It was such a sad story to listen to. I couldn't believe Shalanda survived such a horrible situation in her life, she was a goddamn superhero in my eyes.

After out chat and everyone had gone to bed, I sat up watching TV, thinking about Jayme-Lee and how life could just stop in an instant. It was in that exact moment that I thought, *'What the hell am I doing in South Australia?'* I loved seeing my family, but I hated the cold. I ended up lasting three more weeks in Adelaide before I decided it was time to go home to Darwin. I said see ya later to my family in Adelaide and made my journey back to Darwin. As soon as I arrived back home, I embraced the beautiful dry season weather. *'Now this is what I call winter,'* I thought to myself as I sun-baked out the back of Mum's unit. Simone was very happy to hear I was back in town and it didn't take us long to go back to our normal dinner outings and gossip sessions. Once my friends caught wind that I was back in town, we organised a night out on the town. Tuesday nights were the best nights to go party, there was a pub that held an event called TOT (Tits Out Tuesday).

Basically, girls would get up on stage and flash their boobs and whoever got the loudest cheer won. It was always a good time at TOT, and to be honest, I was usually too drunk to notice anyone getting their boobs out. I did, however, notice a lovely young man at the pub, who I had kissed a couple of times before.

'Hey Matt,' I said.

Matt smiled a rather cheeky smile at me, handed me a shot that he had just ordered at the bar, grabbed my hand and walked me outside, kissed me and said, *'Let's go back to my house'*. We held hands as we stumbled down the street, towards a service station to grab a drink of water. Somehow we managed to become distracted by a car that was parked behind the service station. It had just been washed and I thought it would be a fantastic idea to sit up on the bonnet so I could kiss Matt. I managed to get myself onto the car bonnet in my drunken state but as I sat down on the bonnet, my hands slipped on the freshly washed car. I slid clean off the car and heard an almighty crack. I knew instantly that I had broken my arm. I got up off the ground, looked at Matt who was standing there in shock looking at my arm.

'It's broken isn't it?' I asked Matt.

'Yep it sure is,' Matt answered, as he tried not to vomit.

I held my broken arm up with my other arm and made my way to the service station so I could call an ambulance. I had a quick look at my arm, noticed a big bulge poking out and began to panic. I walked into the service station cradling my arm, approached the man working behind the counter and asked for him to call an ambulance, which he refused to do. I was showing him my arm, yelling that it was broken. He pointed outside towards the back of the building and said, *'That's my car you were just sitting on'*.

I think I was shit out of luck in getting the rather pissed off attendant to help me, so I decided to walk home. It was about a ten-minute sober walk, so I was looking at maybe 20 minutes. I had lost Matt somewhere in the chaos but I had bigger problems to worry about than a drunken one-night stand.

As I was walking home, I walked right into a street full of people fighting. They were using street signs and poles to hit each other with. I was certain I was going to be killed, which left me with no choice but to call Mum and Mike to come and pick me up. I got in the car screaming in agony. Mum couldn't even look at my arm, she just kept telling Mike to hurry up and get me to the hospital. I really didn't enjoy telling Mum how I broke my arm, it was another awkward conversation that I didn't exactly want to have with my mother, but I was too drunk to come up with a lie, so I just told her the truth.

When I arrived at the hospital, the doctors made me sober up before deciding what to do with my arm. I told Mum and Mike to go home as it would be a long wait and they had work in a couple of hours. I sat around for four hours, until finally I had a cast put on and was sent on my way. I had six weeks in the cast, which meant I couldn't get a job anywhere.

But I still applied for jobs and went for interviews. I landed myself one at an adult store, and I was allowed to start as soon as my cast came off. I had never worked in an adult store before, so my first day on the job was a huge eye-opener. I had never seen so many sex toys in my life. It was a crazy job at times, but I enjoyed it. My friends from the casino would come and visit me a lot while I was at work. I loved seeing them and we still made time to get drunk together whenever we could.

One night, Simone and the rest of the casino crew were heading out for a drinking session. I had to work the next day and decided that maybe it was best if I stayed sober. It was funny watching everyone else get drunk, knowing it wasn't going to be me hungover the next day.

Around 3am Simone and I decided it was time to go home. We left the pub, crossed the road and began to walk to a friend's car who was also sober that night. I saw this tall man walking towards me. I smiled and went to step out of his way. He stopped me to tell me I had the most beautiful smile. I laughed and kept walking.

'Can I have your number please? I want to take you on a date,' he begged.

'No way', I said, but this man was persistent.

The whirlwind of narcissism - part 1

I turned to Simone as I was getting in the car and said, *'Watch this'*, I yelled my number out so fast that I knew there was no way this guy would remember it. Simone and I had a good laugh and went on our way.

When I arrived home, I had a shower and tucked myself into bed. As I was slowly dozing off, I heard my phone ding. *'Who the fuck is texting me at this time'* I thought. I opened up the message and it read, *'Hi Jasmin, It's Tom from outside the pub. I remembered your number and saved it in my phone. Can we catch up for a coffee and a chat tomorrow?'*

I almost died when I read the text, I couldn't believe he actually remembered my number. I had shouted it out so quickly, knowing he wouldn't remember it. I didn't know whether to be concerned or impressed. Either way, this Tom guy was obviously keen to hang out, so I decided to agree to a coffee date, but it had to be while I was at work the next day. If I was going to hang out with a random off the street, I wanted it to be in a place where I could hit a panic button under the counter at any time. The following day, Tom stuck to his word and showed up for a chat, but no coffee. He made me a big, healthy lunch instead, which instantly impressed me.

Tom sat and talked to me for hours, in-between me helping customers. Tom and I both shared a passion for music, especially AC/DC. He mentioned he had never been in an adult store before; he was fascinated by all of the adult toys that were on display. As the day went on, Tom told me he had to tell me something. Before he could say another word, I said, *'Is it that you have a son?'*

Tom was stunned. *'How did you know?'* he asked.

'I saw a little baby on your phones screensaver when you opened up your phone, and I just assumed he was your son,' I said.

Tom went on to tell me that he had just moved to Darwin after his wife, Gina, had kicked him out. His son, Liam, was only eight weeks old when Tom left for Darwin, which I thought would have been so hard on Tom – especially after he told me that his ex took all of his personal belongings and left him out on the street.

I learned a lot about Tom that day and he learned a lot about me. Something clicked with us. I enjoyed his company a lot. Once my shift was over, Tom drove me home, and as we pulled up in the driveway he started to tell me how crazy it was that he had met someone as beautiful as me and that he wanted to kiss me. He put one hand on my cheek, leaned in and kissed me. I won't lie, the kiss was horrible, he used way too much tongue, but it didn't stop the fact that Tom was a nice guy, so I agreed to meet up again the next day and the next and the next. Before I knew it, we were dating. I had never

The whirlwind of narcissism - part 1

been in a real relationship with a male before so it took some getting used to and as much as I really liked Tom, I always had my guard up, just that little bit.

Tom ended up moving into Mum's place with me. He showered me with gifts and flowers all the time. It was really sweet and although I wasn't anywhere near as affectionate as Tom, I did appreciate his gestures. Everything seemed to be running smoothly with our relationship until I decided to have a few drinks one sunny afternoon in Darwin. I of course had way too many, which Tom absolutely hated. We ended up having an argument over it, he stormed out and I didn't see him for the rest of the night.

The next day I woke up feeling absolutely horrible. I felt like I had stuffed it all up with Tom. I didn't want to lose him because I had gotten too drunk. I tried to call him all day but he ignored my calls. I decided to let him call me once he was ready, I figured he just needed space. A couple of days went by when Tom finally texted me. He wanted to see me and have a talk; I was afraid he would end things before giving me a fair go. Tom wanted me to head over to the share house he used to live at – apparently that was where he had been staying the past couple of days.

I made my way over to see him. I walked in, sat down on the couch and listened to what he had to say. Tom had asked me to stop drinking, he didn't like it and never wanted to see me drunk again. I felt like maybe he was being over the top, but I wanted the relationship to work so I agreed. After our conversation, I noticed Tom had what looked like a love bite on his neck. It was really small though and I didn't want to start an argument if I was wrong so I didn't say anything, but my gut just didn't feel right after seeing it.

Tom wanted to have a shower before heading back over to my place. He put his phone on the coffee table, told me he would be back in ten and to relax on the couch. As soon as I heard the shower turn on, I looked over at Tom's phone. I knew the passcode but I didn't want to be that partner who snoops in her boyfriend's phone either. My heart was racing, I kept telling myself not to do it, but I just couldn't help myself. I opened the phone, scrolled through his messages and there they were, every last person he had been texting behind my back since we had been together. Turns out he was desperately trying to get his ex back, he was also texting someone he had obviously been cheating on his ex with, and then I got to the girl he had cheated on me with the same night we had an argument. I read all that I needed to, threw his phone back on the table and left. I got home, went to my bedroom and ignored every single call from Tom. He called me at least 25 times in a space of ten minutes. I ended up turning my phone off but he ended up at my house. He knew I had read his messages and wanted to explain himself.

The whirlwind of narcissism - part 1

'How the fuck do you begin to explain something like this?' I thought to myself, as I went outside to listen to the excuses that Tom was about to make. He began to explain his whole relationship with Gina and how he lived a double life, he was seeing another woman behind Gina's back, he had a secret phone, and would find any excuse to leave the house to see this other woman. I was in complete shock, not only at the fact that Tom was a complete bullshit artist, but at the fact that he found the time and energy to do all of this. I had cheated in the past, but this was a whole different level of cheating. Tom then explained that he cheated on me because I started an argument with him and he was hurt by it. I was so hurt that I was being blamed for Tom cheating on me, but the more he said it, the more I believed it. Maybe it was my fault, maybe I was so out of line that Tom was left with no choice but to cheat on me.

After listening to Tom for a good two hours, I decided that I had all the respect in the world for Gina but the very little respect I had for myself was slipping. I was left feeling like I was the person in the wrong and Tom was a victim. I told Tom to leave. I needed space and time to decide if this relationship was worth moving on with. Tom respected my wishes and left.

I spent two days thinking about Tom and the decent man I knew he could be. I turned to Simone for some advice. She was the world's best listener and I knew she would help me make the best decision. Simone was worried about me after I told her everything, but she did say that she couldn't stop me from going back to Tom either. I was so confused, especially when Tom kept messaging me begging for forgiveness. He wanted to make it up to me and silly me ended up caving. I took him back. Tom moved back in with me and we went on with life as if nothing happened, mainly because he wouldn't let me bring up anything to do with his past or cheating on me. Tom asked that I didn't tell anyone about him cheating on me. He didn't know I had told a few people, and there was no way I was going to tell him either. I didn't want another argument, so I lied and said I wouldn't tell anyone.

In a few months I was heading off to America for a girls trip that was organised before Tom was in the picture. Tom kept saying he didn't want me to go, and he asked if I would miss him. My head was saying *'Not really'* but my mouth said, *'Of course I will'*. Tom offered to take me out for dinner two weeks before my trip, and he told me to wear something pretty. I didn't own pretty things, I wore a lot of black. I had a black dress hanging in my wardrobe so I threw that on, straightened my hair and threw on a little bit of make-up, which was a pretty big deal for me. I didn't like make up. I always thought if someone falls in love with me, it will be for my natural beauty and also because I sucked at applying make-up. I came out of the bathroom after getting ready, to find Tom standing there in a suit.

The whirlwind of narcissism - part 1

'What sort of fucking dinner are we going to?' I asked.

'Please don't swear babe, I hate it,' Tom replied as he was finding the car keys. I swore all the time, it was who I was, I was going to struggle with cutting out the F and C bombs that was for sure.

It was the wet season and a storm was brewing. We quickly ran to the car and made our way to a bar near home. Everyone was staring at Tom, because he was in a suit and they were all in shorts and t-shirts. We sat outside in the stinking hot humidity praying for the rain to hit so we could cool down. Tom was being extra sweet, telling me everything a girl loves to hear. We had dinner, a couple of drinks then Tom asked to go for a walk along the beach across the road from the pub. As we got to the beach, the rain came, and we were soaked within seconds. I was asking to leave but Tom insisted we stay, then he got down on one knee, in the pouring rain, opened up a box with a stunning ring inside and asked me to marry him. I couldn't believe it, we had only been together a few months and if you have made it this far in my book, you'll know that our relationship was already a mess. I just stood there, saying nothing at all. Tom must have known I wasn't exactly sure on the whole engagement thing, because he went on to promise me things for the future. The one thing he said that stood out for me was about a family. I was still grieving from my termination. Tom knew that and now that I look back, I think he threw that promise in, knowing it would sell. I ended up saying *'Yes'*. I decided to keep our engagement a secret just until I got back from America, so I only wore the ring at home and didn't take it on the trip.

As soon as I returned from the trip, Tom was waiting at the airport with the ring in his pocket, ready to put it on my finger, so we could tell everyone we were engaged. I wanted to tell Simone in person, so I took her out for dinner a few nights after I returned. I was so nervous to tell her. If I didn't get her approval, I would be devastated. I had the ring on my other hand at first, Simone noticed it and asked if it was an engagement ring, I said *'No'* then changed the subject, but she very quickly turned the conversation back to the ring.

'It looks just like an engagement ring, Jasmin,' Simone said as she stared at me, waiting for me to tell the truth.

'It's an engagement ring Simone,' I said as I waited for her response. Simone got all excited, she hugged me and said congratulations, which made me feel so much better about things. I asked her to be one of my bridesmaids. Simone and I had always said if we got married, we would be each other's bridesmaids and I was sticking to that promise.

As soon as Simone knew, I told everyone else. I made an announcement on social media, and made phone calls to family. Once everyone knew, it was time to set a date. Tom wanted to get married in a few months, I wanted to hold off for a year at least, but Tom was firm on wanting the wedding in a few months, so we decided on a date for that year. 12-12-12 sounded like the perfect date for a wedding, so we set the date, agreed to have the wedding in my hometown of Port Lincoln and began to plan.

I would sit at work Googling everything wedding. I was busy looking at wedding dresses one night when I heard someone walk through the door. I looked up to greet the customer, and I was completely taken back when I saw Lachlan standing in front of me. Lachlan had joined the Navy and was living back in Darwin. As soon as he spoke, it was like every single butterfly in the world had moved into my stomach and was fluttering around. Lachie wanted me to come outside and see his new car. He had spoiled himself with a Holden SS ute. I had a laugh at his number plates – they said NUM NUM. That's what Lachie was called by his dad as a kid, it made no sense to me but Lachie was proud of them. He asked if I wanted his phone number so he could take me for a spin in his car one day. I had never said yes to anything so quickly in my life, and we swapped numbers. *'Holy shit, I have Lachie's number,'* I squealed inside my head. I had forgotten I was engaged and was only looking at wedding dresses ten minutes earlier.

As I was sitting inside Lachie's car, we both noticed a car pull up behind us. I got out, said a quick goodbye to Lachie and started to walk inside, but out of the corner of my eye, I saw Tom walking over to me.

'Who was that?' he asked.

I could tell he was fuming. I explained that it was my mate Lachie, he had just moved back to Darwin and wanted to show me his car. Tom was so angry that I had sat in another man's car. He asked that I don't sit in his car again. He asked if I had Lachie's phone number, I said 'No', but he didn't believe me. Thankfully a group of drunk customers stumbled through the door and began to cause a scene in the shop. Tom took it upon himself to chat to the customers to try to keep them well-behaved, which gave me time to grab my phone and change Lachie's name to a female name. I knew Tom would want to snoop through my phone at some stage, and I had to be one step ahead of him.

After my shift was over and we got home, Tom began to question me about Lachie. *'How long have you known him, have you fucked, does he find you attractive?'* I was put through the ringer. The more questions I was asked, the angrier I got. I felt like a 15-year-old being lectured by her dad, it was weird and I got angry. I began to yell and throw shit across the room. Tom grabbed me to try to settle me down, which just made me angrier, and without a second thought, I slapped him across the face. He was stunned. I stood there waiting to be slapped back but

Tom left. I went to the fridge, grabbed an ice-cold rum, opened it and skulled the whole thing. Tom didn't come home that night. I texted to see if he was ok once I had cooled down, but he didn't respond.

The next day Tom walked through the front door with the biggest black eye I had ever seen.

'What the fuck happened to you?' I said in a panic. I thought he had been in a fist fight.

Tom looked at me with this smug look on his face and said, *'You did this to me when you slapped me'.*

Mum was standing there, and she looked at me confused. She couldn't work out how a slap caused such a huge black eye. I just felt guilt.

'I'm so sorry Tom,' I said.

I didn't think one slap would cause so much damage. I understood if Tom wanted to leave me, I would have left him if it was the other way around, but he didn't leave. He seemed happy just to see me feel so guilty.

Later that day we sat down and started talking about wedding guests. Tom was adamant that he didn't want his family invited. I barely knew his family, they would always argue and stop talking to each other, so I understood why he didn't want them to attend our big day. I always made sure to double check with him over the next few weeks though, just in case he changed his mind, but he answered with the same thing every time – *'NO'*.

As much as I was enjoying buying everything for the wedding, I was noticing that Tom wasn't paying anything towards the wedding, which began to stress me out. I was pouring thousands into it, but when I would ask Tom to pitch in, he made excuses about child support and other bills. In fact I started to notice Tom never had money. This made me wonder how he bought my engagement ring, but I knew not to ask about it. It would only cause an argument.

Simone loved helping with the wedding. She would send me dress ideas all the time, and we went looking for dresses together as well. I ended up choosing two different types, one for the ceremony and one for the reception. During this time I received a large tax return back, which was going to help me a lot with the catering for the wedding. I decided to stuff it in a shoe box of personal items, shoved it at the back of my wardrobe, covered it with my clothes and told Tom to take it to the bank the next day.

The next day rolled around, I got home from work, and asked Tom if he banked the money. He said he didn't have time, but something inside my head told me to check the money. I went into the wardrobe and pulled out the shoe box to discover that the money was gone. I looked at Tom.

'Are you sure you didn't bank the money?' I asked.

'I didn't do it today, I was busy,' Tom replied.

I was instantly mad. Who would steal from us? No one else knew it was there except for Tom, but he was quick to point the finger at my mum's friend who was spending two weeks at our place. I approached Mum's friend, and she denied it straight away. If she didn't take it, then Tom did and I couldn't marry a thief, so I blamed this woman for coming into my room and stealing almost $3000 from me. Once I had finished screaming and yelling, I went back to my bedroom. Tom sat on the bed with tears rolling down his face saying, *'How could she steal from us?'* over and over. I stood there, looking at him, thinking, *'Wow, this is academy award winning stuff right here'*, but I didn't question him about the stolen money. Once again, I didn't want an argument and to be made to feel like an asshole, so I ignored it.

Mum's friend left that night and didn't come back; I guess I scared her off. Mum offered to pay for our catering so that the wedding would still go ahead, which was such a sweet gesture. I didn't see Tom trying to come up with any sort of money though, he just sat back and watched everyone else help pay for our wedding.

It was only a few days before we flew to Port Lincoln. I was having serious cold feet, I wanted to cancel everything. I spoke to Tom about it and I begged to cancel the wedding, but Tom didn't understand why I wanted to and I couldn't understand either. My gut was telling me not to do it, but all I could think was how much of a waste it would be if I cancelled, so we went ahead with the wedding – but not before one last thing made me second guess everything.

I received a message from Lachie saying, *'Are you sure you want to marry this guy?'*

'FUCK BALLS!' I said as I read the message.

I wanted to write back, *'NO I DON'T WANT TO'*, but instead I lied to Lachie and to myself by writing, *'Of course I want to, I love this man'*. But as much as I thought I loved Tom, it wasn't enough to marry him.

On the wedding day, I wasn't nervous at all. Shelby asked me something that always stuck with me. She asked, *'What happens if you fall out of love Jasmin?'*

I responded with, *'Easy, I'll get a divorce'*.

I knew after Shelby asked that question that I was making a mistake. I went and got ready anyway, but the whole time I was secretly screaming on the inside. Once everyone was done up in their make-up and dressed, it was time to go.

The whirlwind of narcissism - part 1

Shelby's brother kindly offered to drive me to the wedding along with my dad. Dad and I laughed and joked all the way there. It was like I was going to someone else's wedding, not my own, until I pulled up at the ceremony where shit got real. I saw Tom standing with his groomsmen, waiting patiently for me to get out of the car.

'Here goes nothing,' I said to Dad as he helped me out of the car.

I had no shoes on. I figured being a beach wedding, I wouldn't need them. As soon as I heard Bryan Adams' *(Everything I do) I do it for you*, I knew it was time to walk. Dad kept telling me to slow down. I was pretty much running down the aisle. I locked eyes with Simone at one point, she looked so happy for me, if only she knew what I was thinking earlier that day. I made it to Tom, we hugged and the ceremony began. We read our own vows, I can't remember one single word I said, or what he said to me. I was just glad when the ceremony was over and we could go and relax at the reception.

Walking into the reception was fun. Pink was playing as Tom, myself and our wedding party all danced over to our table. I was sad to see so many empty chairs at the reception. Lots of people didn't show up for the reception and once the food was out and eaten, people left very quickly. Simone ended up getting wasted, which was hilarious to watch. She was having a blast, and so were the rest of my guests who flew all the way from Darwin to watch me marry Tom.

Dad made a speech towards the end of the night. He was saying how proud he was when I was born and he finally got his little girl. I looked over at Mum when he was saying those beautiful words, and she had the biggest smile on her face. After Dad's speech, the party really died down and it was time to leave. As Tom and I made our way back to our hotel, I kept thinking about what Lachie had asked me only a few days before I was due to get married. I wondered if maybe that was Lachie's way of telling me to not marry Tom and be with him? Whatever Lachie's intentions were though, it was too late now.

Chapter 6

The whirlwind of narcissism – part 2

Tom and I were married for three weeks before we decided to move out of Mum's place. We moved in with a friend of ours, Brandon, and his boyfriend Frank. They had a townhouse and had offered us the bottom half, which we happily accepted.

Tom and I hadn't organised a honeymoon yet but I planned a trip for us to Brisbane to see The Script in concert. We had a great time, singing and dancing the night away. Once the concert was over, Tom and I caught a taxi back to our hotel. The entire trip back, I felt extremely nauseous. The taxi driver was flying through the streets of Brisbane and my stomach just wasn't handling it too well.

'That drive back made me so bloody sick,' I whinged to Tom.

He suggested I just go to bed and sleep it off. The next morning, I woke up feeling much better, we went out for breakfast then made our way to the airport to fly home. The flight was really smooth, but when it was time to land, my nauseous feeling was back. I wasn't the biggest fan of flying – although I flew a lot, I hated the landing part so I figured I had a bit of anxiety which was making me feel sick.

Once we had landed and made our way home, I started to wonder if I was pregnant. I went onto my phone to check my period diary application, when I discovered that I was a day late. I hadn't even noticed I was late; I was too busy having fun in Brisbane. My period was like clockwork, so I was pretty damn sure I was having a baby.

Tom went to the supermarket and bought a 2-pack of pregnancy tests. I did the first one, which didn't show anything at all, not even the control line. Tom told me not to bother taking the other test as it was clear I wasn't pregnant. He got ready to go to the gym, kissed me goodbye and on his way out he said, *'Don't waste your time with the other test Jasmin'.*

I nodded, Tom shut the front door, started the car and drove off. I sat in the bathroom reading the instructions

The whirlwind of narcissism – part 2

to the test when I discovered something I had never read before. I could pee into a cup then dip the test in there. I had no clue about that, I just used to pee straight onto the test. I ran upstairs, found some foam cups, grabbed one, ran back downstairs, peed into the cup and took the test that I was told not to take.

I sat the test down on the bathroom sink and waited. I didn't lecture myself in the mirror this time, I just closed my eyes and hoped for two lines to show up. I felt so sick waiting for those three very long minutes to pass. I was counting the minutes in my head, making sure I wasn't counting too fast, just in case I peeked at the test too early. As soon as the three minutes were up, I kept my eyes shut, felt around the sink for the test, picked it up, lifted it to my face and opened my eyes.

'HOLY SHIT IT'S POSITIVE!' I screamed with excitement.

I ran into the lounge room singing, *'I'm going to be a mum'*. There was no one at home but me, I think I even shouted, *'No one is here with me to celebrate but I don't care, because I'm going to be a mum'*. I tried to call Tom but he wasn't answering. I called Simone, she didn't answer, I called my mum and she answered. I was screaming down the phone, *'Mum don't tell anyone, but I'm pregnant and Tom doesn't know yet, so you can't repeat what I told you'*.

Mum laughed and said, *'Jasmin you're yelling that loud that Mike can actually hear what you're saying'*. Oops, me and my big mouth.

'Ok well, you both can't say anything,' I said, in a much quieter voice. I hung up the phone from Mum and thought I would surprise Tom with the positive test. I knew he would come home from the gym and have a shower straight away, so I wrote on a piece of paper, *'You're going to be a daddy'* with the test stuck to the paper. I then stuck the paper on the mirror.

I sat and waited very impatiently for Tom to arrive home. I heard his car pull up and lay on the couch pretending I was really fixated on the TV show I was watching. Tom walked in, said *'Hello'* then made his way to the shower. I was holding my breath waiting for him to come racing out straight away, but he didn't. I heard the shower turn on, he had his shower, the shower turned off and still no word from Tom. I wondered if he hadn't seen the note yet, but he couldn't have missed it, it was smack bang in the middle of the mirror.

Tom ended up coming out after what felt like an eternity, sat down on the couch and started scrolling through his phone. I asked if he had seen the note in the bathroom, he looked at me really confused.

'No, what note?' he asked.

The whirlwind of narcissism – part 2

I got up, took him by the hand, walked him into the bathroom and showed him the note. He read it, turned to me, cuddled me and said, *'Oh, you're pregnant, so you took the test after I told you not to'*.

I was stunned at his response. I was waiting for some sort of excitement to come from him, but there was nothing. I asked if he was happy, he shrugged his shoulders and said, *'Yeah, it's good'*. I was left feeling like my pregnancy was already a burden on this man. I didn't say another word to him for the rest of the night.

The next day, Simone called me. I told her the news and she was so excited and happy for me. I told her about Tom's reaction, which she also found really weird. In fact, after I told him the news about us having a baby, Tom's whole attitude changed for good. We were arguing more, about the smallest things. He would accuse me of sleeping with our roommates, even though they were gay. Apparently I was having sex with them both. He would throw off hints that he wasn't the father – he even went to my mother and told her that he just doesn't understand how I got pregnant. My mum would say, *'You had sex, that's how'*.

At eight weeks pregnant, Tom and I got into a pretty heated argument about Lachie. He had accused me of sleeping with him and said that Lachie was actually the father of the baby, not Tom. I just couldn't take it anymore.

I grabbed my car keys and went to walk out the door. Tom stood in front of me trying to rip the keys from my hand. As we fought over the keys, I ended up behind the back door trying to push the door shut, while Tom was standing outside. I went to shut him out when he kicked the door back open. It swung hard and the door handle hit me straight into the stomach, winding me. Tom walked in, saw me on the ground, grabbed the keys to his car and left. I pulled my phone from my pants pocket and called Simone. I told her everything, and she suggested going to the hospital.

'I will be there soon,' she said.

I got up, went out the front and waited for Simone to pull up.

'You can just drop me off, I know you have work tomorrow,' I said to Simone, but she was more than happy to stay with me.

I was seen by a doctor straight away, and as I was telling the doctor what had happened, he looked at me and said, *'You do know I have to call the police. This is a form of domestic violence.'*

I asked the doctor not to report it because I didn't want to upset Tom but the doctor was left with no choice.

The whirlwind of narcissism – part 2

While I was waiting for the police to arrive, I had an ultrasound to check on the baby. Simone and I watched this little baby moving around in my belly. We looked at each other smiling away.

'Getting clucky are ya Simone?' I joked.

'I'm happy to be aunty Simone for now,' she joked back.

Once I was told that the baby was fine, I told Simone I was leaving before the police arrived.

We quickly left through the A&E doors, and just as we walked out, the police were walking in. They looked at me, but I put my head down and kept walking. I'm guessing I looked suspicious because they ended up following me, yelling out my name. The two officers pulled me aside to question me. I made it sound like it was my fault, I told them Tom accidentally kicked the door into me, not realising I was there. They wrote everything down and sent me on my way.

'Why did you lie?' Simone asked.

I didn't want anyone thinking Tom was a bad person, so I put the blame on myself.

Simone asked if I wanted to sleep at her and Cody's house for the night.

'I'm ok, you know I'm tough,' I said as I got out of the car.

I thanked Simone for being there for me, said goodnight and went inside. Tom was there waiting. He had no idea I had been up at the hospital. When I told him, he didn't seem to care. He fully denied kicking the door into my stomach.

'You did Tom, you were the only person standing on the other side of the fucking door. The police were called, they want to speak to you,' I told him.

'You called the police on your own husband, what sort of person are you?' Tom lectured me. 'Who knows about our fight?'

I explained that Simone took me to the hospital and she was the only one of my friends who knew.

'Simone will tell everyone, you and her are gossip queens,' Tom snapped. I promised Tom I would make sure Simone wouldn't tell anyone else, I even texted her in front of him asking her to keep it between us. Simone reassured me she wouldn't tell a soul. Tom eventually calmed down. He never apologised for what had happened but he wasn't angry anymore, so I decided to drop the whole conversation and go to bed. It was 2am and I was knackered.

The whirlwind of narcissism – part 2

Over the next few weeks, my morning sickness kicked in. I would spew morning, noon and night but it was nowhere near as bad as my first pregnancy, so there was no complaining from me. The complaining was coming from Tom. I would vomit in the toilet throughout the night, which woke Tom up. He would come into the toilet and tell me to shut up. I felt guilty every time I spewed, I didn't want to upset Tom, but I just couldn't help it. Tom would tell me that he held Gina's hair back and rubbed her back while she spewed during her pregnancy so I assumed he would do the same for me, but that never happened, which made me feel worthless for some reason.

Although my sickness was bad, I still went to work. I wanted to tell the world I was pregnant, Tom wasn't very keen but after a few weeks of me pestering him, he let me announce it on social media. Tom hated social media, he always tried to turn me against it, but I enjoyed sharing my life with my friends. Lachie had seen the announcement and said congratulations in the comments. Tom took one look at that and was furious.

'See, he is the father isn't he?' he snapped. I just rolled my eyes.

A couple of weeks went by. One day, I was at home on the couch and I noticed Brandon walk through the door. Usually he would smile and chat to me, but this time he walked straight past me without saying a word.

It was very odd for Brandon to ignore me; I was trying to tell myself that maybe he had a shit day but I could just feel that he was angry at me.

Tom came through the door five minutes later in a huff. I asked what was wrong, and he told me that as he was driving to work that day, a black SS ute tried to run him off the road.

'Maybe it was your crappy driving,' I joked.

Tom asked if any of my friends owned a black SS ute. I couldn't think of anyone, forgetting that Lachie owned one. The next day Tom walked in from work really angry.

'I found out who is trying to run me off the road,' he said, and before I could ask who, he said, *'It's Lachie'*.

I instantly didn't believe him. He said he had seen the the number plates this time which said NUM NUM. Tom knew Lachie's number plates from the night he pulled up behind him at the adult store. I could clearly see he was lying. He went on and on about me never speaking to him again, but I refused. I ended up packing up some clothes that afternoon and going to stay with my mum. I needed a break from Tom.

Tom texted me every day, begging for me to come home. Eventually I caved and went back. When I arrived home,

The whirlwind of narcissism – part 2

our part of the house was spotless. It felt nice coming back to a clean home. I wasn't as clean as I usually was during the pregnancy, the sickness would always get the better of me. One day Tom had me go upstairs with him to make some lunch, and as we got to the kitchen, I noticed a note in the toaster, so I picked it up and read it. Brandon had written a note that had said that he isn't a maid so I need to start cleaning up my own mess. I looked at Tom very confused, I had been at Mum's for three days, so I wasn't even there to make a mess. No one was home to talk to about it, so I wrote a note back. I had told Brandon that I was trying my best to keep everything clean and if he wanted to speak about anything from now on, come and speak to me in person. Tom looked at the note, snatched it from me and ripped it up. He didn't want me responding to the note at all. I asked if I was seriously that messy, Tom looked me dead in the eye and said, *'You are a fucking slob'*.

All I could say was *'Sorry'*. I felt so guilty. Tom opened up his phone to show me messages from Brandon. Brandon was telling Tom that I was close to being kicked out because of my anger outbursts and laziness. He wouldn't show me any other messages, only the ones he wanted me to see. I had a feeling that Tom had been telling Brandon a few little white lies about me, that's why he had started to distance himself from me and was leaving notes. Thankfully the lease was up in two weeks and we were able to move out. Mum had allowed us to move back with her and Mike so we could save for a rental once the baby was born.

I was glad to get out of Brandon's house. I felt like I was never welcome there in the end, so going home to Mum's was great. My sickness slowly faded once I was 16 weeks along. I was going in for a scan at 17 weeks but had said I didn't want to find out the gender until my baby shower. I wanted to be just as surprised as my friends when the gender reveal cake was cut. Tom was going to find out the gender and not tell me, but that all went out the window once we arrived to our scan. I had told the sonographer about my plan to find out the gender at my baby shower. The sonographer was a cheeky one – she started telling me I should find out the gender and just surprise my friends instead. I looked over at Tom, who was standing there gritting his teeth, death staring me. I looked back over at the sonographer and said, *'Your idea sounds much better, tell me the gender too'*.

She got down to the genital area, smiled at me and said, *'It's a boy'*. I was ecstatic. I had always said I never wanted a daughter; I had been a teenager and I didn't want a mini me, at all. Tom had his fake smile on as I cleaned all of the gel from my stomach. We got our cute little scan photos then made our way to the car. I was on a complete high. I was having a son. That high came crashing down as soon as Tom and I got in the car. He began his normal lecture, asking why I had found out the gender, how selfish I was for not sticking to the plan and ruining his moment for him. I sat in the car with my head down listening to the man who I married, telling me off for finding out the gender of our baby.

His lecture worked though. I was made to feel guilty, so fucking guilty.

As time went on, Tom started to become very controlling. I was told who I could and couldn't speak to, and if I wasn't at work, I was to be home, in the bedroom. I was told when I could shower, and once I had sent my condolences to Lachie when his dad passed away, I was made to delete social media as well. I was stronger than most women I knew, but this man had me so controlled that I just did as I was told. Mum noticed I was always in my room. She would pop her head in to see if I was ok, I would lie and say I was fine when really, I was dying on the inside. My only escape was work but if I worked an afternoon shift, Tom would sit with me the entire time, just in case anyone came in to visit me.

He would sit there telling me that he was probably better off raising our son, who he wanted to name 'Noah'. He would tell me that my temper was so bad that he didn't trust me alone with the baby and I would probably end up killing my son. Every day I would hear this sort of stuff come out of Tom's mouth and anyone who's been in a relationship like this, knows that you start to believe the things that are being drilled into your head. I put up with it until I exploded; I was standing at work, yelling at Tom. I was telling him to fuck off out of my life, I just couldn't stand him any longer. Tom marched up to me, his nose was touching mine, and he said, *'Come on Jasmin, hit me, punch me as hard as you can'.*

I took a step back, looked Tom square in the eyes and headbutted him right on his nose. Tom ran off outside, crying. I sat down on the ground, taking deep breaths and trying to relax my heart that was beating out of my chest. Tom walked back in, blood pouring from his face, and handed me his phone to look at the pictures he just took of himself with a busted nose.

'See why I have no faith in you being a good mother?' Tom said, as he wiped blood from his nose.

I was convinced that night. I was convinced that I would have our son, hand him over to Tom and leave. My son deserved better, and so did Tom.

By the time I was seven months pregnant, I had noticed that almost all of my friends that I met when I first started at the casino had either stopped talking to me, or I had managed to push them away.

Simone was still in my life, but only just. We barely saw each other anymore. I missed her so much but Tom made sure I only saw her when he said it was ok.

The whirlwind of narcissism – part 2

I also had my good friend Dion; he had previously worked at the casino but recently moved to Ceduna in South Australia to work at the local supermarket. We would chat on the phone, mainly when Tom was at work and the entire time I would be listening out for Tom's car to pull in the driveway. If he had caught me talking to Dion, I would be the biggest whore on the planet.

Tom was even starting to try and control my own mum. He was telling her what she could and couldn't do in her own home, which led to them having an argument. Mum ended up telling Tom that he had to move out, which meant that Tom was going to drag me out with him.

We had nowhere else to go in Darwin, and Tom left it up to me to find a roof over our heads. He gave me a week to find something. I searched all over Darwin for rentals but everything was so expensive. Tom mentioned going to the Sunshine Coast, so I googled houses there, but we had the same issue – everything was overpriced. Tom mentioned Dion in Ceduna.

'Why don't we ask Dion if he can get me a job with him in Ceduna,' he suggested.

'I can ask him,' I replied.

I grabbed my phone, called Dion and asked him if he could get Tom a job. Thankfully there was a position available and Dion offered us a rental he had in Ceduna. I hung up the phone, looked at Tom and said, *'Looks like we are off to Ceduna'*.

I really didn't want to go. Although Ceduna was really close to Port Lincoln, I knew I was going to be completely alone when I had the baby. Tom booked a cheap removalist and we began to pack up our things. As we were packing up our bed, I lifted up the mattress and noticed a butter knife that had fallen out from the mattress.

'Why is there a knife stuffed under the bottom of our mattress?' I asked Tom.

Tom snatched the knife from me and snapped, *'I don't know Jasmin, just pack'*.

'I think he's going to kill me,' I thought. I definitely didn't want to go anywhere with this man now, but Mum was no longer speaking to Tom or me at this stage. I had no one to turn to in Darwin anymore, so I guess my time there was done.

At 2am the next morning, we left Darwin. On our way out the front door, Mum was sitting on the couch in the lounge room, drinking her tea before an early start at work. She didn't even look at us as we walked out, she didn't even know where I was going.

The whirlwind of narcissism – part 2

As we drove out of Darwin, I felt so sad. I said goodbye to Simone in my head. *'I will miss you,'* I thought to myself as Tom held my hand, promising me this was our fresh start.

It took two days to get to Ceduna, and as we rolled into town, we met Dion at the beach so he could show us where our house would be. I was so happy to see a friendly face. I looked up to Dion a lot and I felt a lot safer knowing we would be living near him. The next day Dion asked Tom if he wanted to go out for a few drinks at the bowls club. I wasn't very keen on going so I decided to stay behind, but before they left, I asked Tom if I could please log back into my social media account. Dion looked at me rather confused.

'Who would have thought you would ask permission to do something Jazzy,' he joked, but I could see the concern in his eyes. Tom was trying to pretend like I didn't have to ask him permission.

'Of course you can, you don't need to ask,' he said, which probably meant, you are going to pay for that later, but I didn't care. I was lonely and missing some sort of contact with my friends.

The boys eventually left for the bowls club while I snuggled up in bed with my phone. I heard Dion's car pull up maybe two hours later. The car was turned off, but no one got out for ages. I ended up getting out of bed and going outside to check on the boys. Tom saw me coming, wound down his window and said, *'Go back to bed, we are just chatting'*. I looked over at Dion, who had the weirdest smile on his face. I knew something was up but I had been told to go back to bed so that's where I went.

After almost two hours of the boys being in the car, Dion went to his other rental he had. He said he wanted to give us our own space and not be in our faces all the time, but I had a feeling that the conversation that just took place upset Dion. Tom ventured inside and began hugging me, rubbing my belly, telling me he loved me more than anything and couldn't wait to be a father. It was so nice that it made me feel awkward as all hell. Tom hopped into bed with me, and we cuddled until we went to sleep.

The next morning, Tom, myself and Dion decided to go fishing. I knew Dion would tell me what was said in his car the night before, but I knew Tom wouldn't allow me to drive to the beach with Dion. I had to go in our car. As we drove to the beach, I noticed one of our fishing rods was broken, which meant Tom had to go and buy a new one. We drove back through town, with Dion driving in front of us to show us where the camping store was.

We ended up parked right next to each other. I got out of the car with Tom but he said to wait where I was, he wanted to run in on his own, which meant I had two minutes to spare. As soon as Tom ran into the shop, I

The whirlwind of narcissism – part 2

opened up Dion's passenger side door. I didn't get in, but I told him to tell me everything that was said. What I heard was absolutely brutal. Dion began to tell me that Tom told him all about the baby not being his. Tom had told Dion that Lachie was 100% the father. He also tried to pay Dion $50 to have sex with me so he had a reason to leave me. I felt sick to my fucking stomach after hearing only a couple of things that he said. Dion never got to tell me the full story, but that's all I needed to hear. Dion kept saying, *'You need to leave him Jasmin, he is destroying you and you deserve better'*. I told Dion I wouldn't say anything to Tom.

I went out fishing with them as if nothing was said, then I went home, had a shower and waited for Tom to start his afternoon shift at work. Tom must have sensed something was up with me, because when he left for work, he locked me inside. The back door was permanently deadlocked and unusable, and Tom left with the only key to the house, which he would use to lock the screen on the front door from the outside so I was shut in.

'Too bad if a fire starts' I said to myself as Tom drove off.

I made a call to Shelby to vent my hurt. Shelby offered to come and kill Tom for me, which was sweet of her, but it just wasn't worth the jail time, so we came up with a secret plan. I had to convince Tom to move to Adelaide. I needed to make him think it would be more stable there for us and I was going to get him more work. If I could do this, I would be surrounded by family. I texted my stepmum and told her that we were thinking of going to Adelaide, and she offered us a room until we got on our feet. She said to come now if I wanted to, but I was almost due and didn't want to drive to Adelaide and risk going into labour.

I wasn't sure if the plan would work. Tom knew my family were in Adelaide and I had learned by now that he didn't want any family around me, but I was willing to give it a shot. I had nothing left to try.

On Christmas Day, I decided to start talking about the idea of moving.

'Doesn't Lachie live in Adelaide?' Tom asked.

'I don't think so,' I answered knowing full well he was there but I wasn't about to fuck up the chance to escape Tom. I mentioned that I could help him get a better paying job, that my family would help us out and we would be so much happier. Tom liked the idea of having a better job. His hours at the supermarket weren't that great and for some reason, he decided he didn't like Dion anymore. I asked him why and all I got was, *'Because the asshole is in love with you'*. I shook my head; I just didn't want to hear his bullshit anymore.

The whirlwind of narcissism – part 2

Boxing Day arrived and so did some serious lower back pain for me. I was trying my best not to complain about it, I knew that labour was going to be worse than a little bit of back pain. As the days went on, my back pain got worse. I was getting up all through the night, holding my back as I went to the toilet. Tom would get angry with me for waking him up by turning on the toilet light. He would bitch and moan at me, toss and turn over and over, making sure I knew I had woken him up and kept him up.

'You better not have this baby before January 1st,' Tom would tell me; he wanted his son to be the first baby born in Ceduna for the year. I knew that was impossible, I was already in early stages of labour and by 1am on the 29th December, I woke Tom up to take me to the hospital.

I was warmly greeted by the midwife, Jenny. She had told me I was in early stages of labour; I was 2cm dilated but my water hadn't broken yet. Jenny offered for us to sleep the night, there was no one else in the maternity ward, so we took her up on that offer. Jenny handed me a sleeping pill, I took it, snuggled in, feeling safe knowing I was in the hospital and went to sleep. Tom had a bed made up on a fold out sofa, far away from me, which I was extremely happy with.

The next morning, I got up and started to walk around the hospital, which Jenny had told me could help with my labour. After a few laps, I was puffed. I went to the toilet and as I pulled my pants down I noticed the tiniest trickle of fluid trickling down my leg, I knew it wasn't wee but it was such a small amount, there was no way it could have been my waters. I yelled out to Jenny, but her shift had finished. Another midwife walked in, Von was her name. I had met Von before at one of my check-ups, she was a stern but nice lady, so I was relieved to see her. Von got me to wear a pad for half an hour so she could swab the fluid and see if it was my waters that had broken. Turns out it was definitely my waters. I was in complete shock, I expected a pool of water to gush out of me, but Von explained that not every woman had that experience and I was glad I didn't to be honest.

Von asked if it was ok if we sped up my labour. I looked over at Tom, who was sitting on the chair with his head buried in his phone.

'What's that involve?' Tom questioned Von.

'Well, I'll put a drip in Jasmin's hand which has Pitocin in it, this well help Jasmin's labour progress quicker, which means baby will be here sooner.'

Tom gave me the nod of approval. I agreed to the Pitocin and Von made it happen. Once the drip was in, I received a call from Dad – he was on his way to Ceduna. He wanted to meet the baby as soon as he was born. I was delighted when he told me he was coming. Tom was absolutely

The whirlwind of narcissism – part 2

livid though, he was saying hurtful things like, *'Why is he coming here? He has never been in your life.'*

As I sat on the bouncy ball, feeling the pains in my back getting stronger, I felt like I wasn't even allowed to be happy on the day I was giving birth. I felt like every moment had to be miserable for me in Tom's eyes, which led me back to the agreement I made with Tom about giving the baby to him once he was born and I would just walk away. I still thought that I would never be a good mother. I still wanted to hand my son over to Tom and then disappear, it was for the best. Suddenly, my pains intensified, I was hurting a lot. Von offered some pain relief, which again, I had to ask Tom if I was allowed to have. He wanted me to have a drug free birth, which I agreed to, until I actually felt labour, then I changed my mind. I asked to try the gas to begin with.

'Of course honey,' Von said as she stroked my hair. *'I will organise that now.'*

Von left the room, I moved off of the ball and onto the bed. Tom walked over to me and said, *'The gas is fine, but you will not be having any epidural. If Gina can go without drugs, you can too.'*

I prayed the gas was going to be really good because I was pushing my luck with Tom just by having the gas. Von returned with the gas, gave me a quick rundown on how to use it, and let me suck down the gas whenever I needed to.

As the hours went by, my contractions became really close together. I begged Tom for an epidural, which was very quickly declined. The gas was doing nothing but making me feel like I had smoked a bag of weed. I was getting on the ball, bouncing, back to the bed, back to the ball and back to the damn bed. Nothing was taking the pain away, not even Dad when he walked in to see how I was doing. Tom shook Dad's hand, let Dad say hello to me then told Dad he would call him once I had the baby. I wanted Dad to stay but he was shuffled out the door so quickly, I didn't even get to ask. Tom had taken my phone away from me hours earlier, I didn't even know where it was, and I didn't care at this stage. Von kept coming in and out checking on me all day. It got to 7:30pm when she checked how far dilated I was.

'Surely I'm 7 or 8 centimetres by now,' I said to Von.

She looked at me and said, *'You are still only 2 centimetres dilated'*.

'You've got to be fucking kidding me,' I whinged.

Von left the room and returned with a doctor. I was watching them both whispering in the corner.

The whirlwind of narcissism – part 2

'Is something wrong with my baby?' I asked.

Von assured me that everything was fine. The doctor introduced himself to me as Dr Manning. He was quietly spoken so as he was talking to me, I would stop him mid-sentence whilst I had a contraction, then once the contraction was over with, I allowed him to continue to talk. Dr Manning spoke to me about a C-section. I wasn't dilating at all, it had been hours and hours and I think maybe the doctor was concerned, although he didn't show it. I agreed to the C-section immediately, I just couldn't take any more pain.

Dr Manning went off to surgery to prepare for my C-section. As Von was prepping me with my cute white stockings and the catheter that hurt like a son of a bitch, I heard a woman screaming through the halls of the hospital. She was in labour and heading straight for an emergency C-section, which meant I had to wait. In my head I was thinking *'FUCK'* but on the outside I was trying my best to remain calm and just get through the pain.

A couple of hours later Von told me it was time to go to theatre. I begged to take the gas with me. Von had a good laugh when I asked her.

'The gas doesn't stretch that far my love,' she said as she was giggling away.

As soon as I was in theatre and had the spinal block put in, the pain was gone. Tom had to wait outside until my spinal block had been done, and once he walked in, I kept saying how I couldn't feel a damn thing from the waist down. It was a strange feeling but it also meant no more contractions. As Dr Manning sliced my belly open I just laid there chatting away to Tom and the team of nurses and doctors. Then I felt a really hard tugging, like all of my insides were being pulled out. I was told that my son was almost here. I was smiling from ear to ear waiting to be told he was born.

At 9:20pm on December 29th, I heard my son, my very first-born baby, cry for the first time. It wasn't a scream or a cry that went on and on, he just let out the tiniest cry, just to let me know he was here. Tom went over to meet our son. He cut the cord, waited for the midwife to wrap the baby up then brought this tiny, beautiful little baby over to me to say 'hello'. I remember seeing him for the first time, he looked right at me and I said, *'Hello my baby boy'*. I remember thinking how cute he was and that Tom and I created such a perfect baby. Von looked at Tom and asked if we had chosen a name for our son. I thought Tom would have said Noah but he said, *'Oh look, Jasmin did all the hard work so she can name him I guess'*.

I looked at Von and said, *'His name is Hudson'*. I had always loved that name, and I never liked Noah, so I'm glad Tom left it up to me to name Hudson.

The whirlwind of narcissism – part 2

As I held Hudson whilst I was stitched up and wheeled back to the recovery room, I thought, *'You are the reason I will leave this shitty relationship, and there's no way in hell that I'm giving you up'.*

After a few days in hospital, Hudson and I were given the all clear to leave. Hudson breastfed well, slept well, and was just a happy little baby. I would text Simone daily updates of Hudson, which she just loved. Tom was really clingy with Hudson though. He would drag the bassinet into the loungeroom at night time and sleep in there with him, while I was left in the bedroom, alone. I would come out to check on Hudson and be told to go back to bed. It was bringing me down a little bit – I wanted to bond with Hudson but the only time I could really hold him was when I breastfed him.

One afternoon I was on the bed breastfeeding Hudson. I went to get up off the bed and hit my toe on the bedside table. I yelled out *'Cunt'* as I semi-hopped around in pain, whilst holding Hudson. I heard Tom come storming down the hallway. He snatched Hudson from me and yelled, *'Don't you ever swear with my son in your arms again'.*

'I was still feeding the baby,' I said as Tom walked back to the lounge room.

'Get out of this house Jasmin, and come back when you learn not to swear.'

I don't know why I did this, but I actually left. I think I had been left feeling so crap, that I just listened without arguing and walked out. As I limped through the streets of Ceduna holding my very fresh wound in my stomach, I kept wondering where to go. I left my phone behind, so I couldn't call Dion. It began to rain and I was about 20 minutes from home. I was in agony from walking so far, so I decided to head home. As I walked through the door, Tom didn't even look at me but I did see formula on the table and bottles. Tom went out while I was walking around and bought formula so he could feed Hudson. He said I could still breastfeed but only during the day. I couldn't even decide when I fed my fucking son. I was furious. I was more than ready to move to Adelaide.

A few days later we moved. Tom was more than happy to leave Ceduna – it meant I left Dion behind. I never got to say goodbye to him and he didn't get to meet Hudson, which broke my heart but I understood, he absolutely hated Tom by this stage and it was best if we just texted each other 'goodbye'.

Once we got to Adelaide and settled in, Tom's behaviour became really odd, especially when I breastfed. He would call me a slut and a whore if I breastfed in front of my family and I was never allowed to breastfeed in public, so if we were out and Hudson was hungry, too bad for Hudson. He had to wait. My sister Shalanda would watch Tom's every move and the way he treated me. She had

The whirlwind of narcissism – part 2

been in a very similar relationship to me and she would tell me that Tom was too controlling, which I knew but I felt scared to leave Tom now. Tom had Hudson any chance he could, he had convinced me to completely stop breastfeeding by this stage. I had never even bathed my son, in my eyes I didn't know how to be a mum. Thankfully Dad had come home for a holiday while we were staying at his house. I knew it was my only chance to get away from Tom. Dad was a kind man but if he got angry, you got out of his way.

One late afternoon, Dad and my stepmum went to a BBQ. I was left alone with Tom and Hudson and I just knew there was going to be trouble. I wanted to sit Tom down and break up with him in front of my dad but I had a funny feeling that wasn't going to happen. Tom was sitting on the couch playing with Hudson when I asked to have a snuggle. Tom said *'No'*. I closed my eyes, opened them again and said, *'He's my son too and I want to bond with him!'* which very quickly escalated into an argument. Tom would call me a whore, I would call him a piece of shit. The names were just flying back and forth.

I went into the bedroom to cool down, but Tom followed, he dumped Hudson onto our bed, grabbed me by the throat and told me to shut my mouth. As he let go, he stormed into the lounge room. Hudson was screaming, I got my phone from my pocket and called Dad.

'Dad I think he might kill me; he is going to fucking kill me,' I screamed down the phone. Tom came back into the bedroom but it was too late. Dad knew what was happening at his house. Dad was too far away but before I hung up, I heard him say, *'I will get someone over there now'*.

Tom heard every word that Dad had yelled into the phone; he knew someone was coming to get me and it scared him. He walked towards me and I ran as fast as I could into the lounge room. I tripped over the rug on my way into the lounge room, and as I rolled over onto my side, Tom walked over to me, and ever so calmly kicked me right in my freshly cut scar. As he walked out the front door he said, *'You win Jasmin'*. I got myself up, locked the lounge room door, and limped into the bedroom where Hudson was still crying on the bed. I picked him up and whispered, *'It's ok now, everything is ok,'* and just like that, Hudson stopped crying.

Tom drove away just as help arrived for me; he escaped a beating that day.

The day after Tom left, I called Mum. We hadn't spoken since I left Darwin, so I gave her a really quick rundown on everything that had happened with Tom and I. Mum suggested I come home to Darwin, which I was happy to say *'yes'* to. Mum booked Hudson and I a flight, we said goodbye to our family in Adelaide, got on a plane and went home.

The whirlwind of narcissism – part 2

Getting home and finding out the lies that Tom was telling my friends and family behind my back really hurt. It also solved a few things I had always wondered about. The knife I found under the bed when we were leaving Darwin, I think he may have planted it there. He had told my mother that he was afraid I was going to stab him in his sleep, so that's the only thing I can think of as to why there was a knife under our bed. He had also confessed to Dion that I never gave him the black eye when I slapped him. He ended up in a fight with a random drunk after he stormed off the night we had the argument. I will never know why Tom was the way he was, I am just so glad we called it quits before someone really did get hurt.

Tom left the day of our argument at Dad's and never returned; he hasn't seen Hudson since he was ten weeks old. Some say he's an asshole, some say I was the asshole. I just say, *'Thank you for giving me such a precious baby'* – I can't fault either of us for that.

Chapter 7

Out of the friend zone

Arriving back in Darwin with Hudson was the best feeling in the world. I was actually able to bathe and cuddle him, I was so excited. My milk had dried up after Tom had told me to stop breastfeeding, which made me feel sad, because I absolutely loved breastfeeding Hudson. It was 'our time', but not to worry, Hudson loved formula just as much. Settling back in at Mum's was nice too, I felt free to roam the house and not be locked away in my bedroom. I called Simone to tell her I was back and she could meet Hudson; she fell in love with him instantly. Simone was always a clucky girl, but she wasn't ready to have her own just yet. Her and Cody had just gotten engaged and she asked me to be a bridesmaid. I was so excited; I felt so honoured to be a part of her special day.

As the weeks passed, I started to feel really motivated. Hudson was such a great baby, he slept beautifully at night which meant I did too. I was sitting on the couch with Hudson one afternoon, I looked down at my rather beautiful Mummy tummy, and thought, *'I think it's time I got rid of you'*.

I put Hudson down for a nap, asked Mum to keep an ear out for him, put my sneakers on and went for a walk. I hadn't exercised in a very long time, so I kept it nice and steady. I found a nice path down the esplanade in the city, which I followed to the very end. At the end was a set of stairs, loads of them, so I figured I would walk down them, walk back up and head home. I was so proud of myself, and it made me feel good. I ended up buying some headphones to plug into my phone, so I could listen to music when I went walking. The next day I walked back to the stairs and walked two laps of them, the day after was three laps, and this went on until I was actually running up and down the stairs. Every day I would head to the stairs, music blaring, heart pounding, sweat pouring down my face, and the whole time I was thinking about Hudson. I had to be his mum and his dad. I had to be fit, healthy, strong.

Slowly I started changing my eating habits. I would eat chicken and vegetables, and if I went out for dinner, I ordered a salad. I was changing my entire life.

Before I knew it, I was doing almost 20 laps a day on the esplanade stairs. I lost over 20kg and I felt like for the first time in my life, I had control over my body, not someone else.

I got myself a part time job at a small supermarket to earn extra money. I worked in the late afternoons, only for a few hours, so Mum was happy to watch Hudson while I worked. Every Sunday, Simone and I would go for lunch and chat about everything that happened during the week. All in all, I would say that life was going really well and I was happily single.

Then one night, only a couple of days after Hudson turned one, I was in bed, scrolling through social media when I saw a message pop up on my phone. It was from Lachlan. I honestly thought to myself, *'Here we go again'*. Lachlan was now living in Perth, he had been posted there with the Navy, and he had just split up with his partner. He felt a little down, so I did the friend thing and gave some advice. Although it was sad that he split from his partner, I was also kind of excited.

We had always had other people or other things going on in our lives, so we didn't get to take a chance on each other. I think I may have even mentioned to Lachlan that I was happy he was single and he deserved better, hoping he would take the hint that I meant he should be with me, but also I didn't want him to get the hint, because I was happily single and had a child to focus on.

Lachlan had told me that he may be getting posted back to Darwin. I played it cool and wrote, *'Oh wow, you must miss the heat hey,'* when in fact I actually wanted to write *'EEEEEEKKKKK'*.

Lachlan and I had never spoken over the phone before. We had known each other for years and only messaged each other, so I was shocked when Lachlan called my phone one afternoon. I looked at his name pop up, which had been changed from a girl's name back to his actual name, and I froze for a second. I didn't want to answer it, but I don't know why. I closed my eyes, took a breath, and hit answer and I'm glad I did. Although Lachlan wasn't big on talking over the phone, he helped keep the conversation going. I could hear in his voice that he wasn't a young 18-year-old anymore, he was a man, which made me curious. I had seen pictures of him on social media, but nothing overly new so I wanted to see his face, in person.

Lachlan had mentioned that he wouldn't be posted back to Darwin until March. It was only January and as much as I promised myself that I needed to stay single, I also wanted to take a chance with this man. I had spoken about coming to visit. Lachlan was very lovely and offered me a bed at his house if I wanted to come and see him. I was just so confused whether or not to book the flights; I was afraid that I would get to Perth and we wouldn't be the same in person as we were on the phone or messages, so I decided not to book the tickets.

Later on that night I was sitting on the couch listening to music, when all of a sudden *Imagine Dragons* came on. The first lyrics to their song 'On Top of the World' made me realise I could potentially lose my chance to ever see whether Lachlan and I would ever have a future together. I grabbed my laptop, went online and booked the flight to Perth. I would be there from Friday afternoon, and leave early Sunday morning. It was a very short trip, but I knew I had to do it.

Lachlan was shocked and so happy that I decided to fly to Perth. Mum had agreed to watch Hudson for me while I was gone. I had spent almost a year being single, which meant I probably needed to shave my legs before I went anywhere. I also needed a couple of pretty dresses to take with me, which Simone helped me pick out at the local surf shop.

Simone was so encouraging of my choice. She was there the day I first saw Lachlan, so she understood why I was going. After a nerve-wracking three day wait, I was on the plane to Perth. I was having the worst anxiety throughout the flight. I remember thinking about asking the pilot to just turn the plane back around, but I knew there was no way I could get out of this. I just had to sit back and try to enjoy the flight.

As the plane was landing in Perth, I started to relax a little more. I figured, *'Hey, if he's a dickhead, I'll just leave, simple'.* I grabbed my bag off the plane, thanked the flight attendant for a great flight and made my way to the pick-up area, where I knew Lachlan was waiting. As I made my way outside, I saw his car pulling up. My heart was thumping through my chest. *'What if he's a serial killer?'* I suddenly questioned myself, but I quickly removed that thought from my mind. I wasn't opening that door now that I was only seconds away from seeing Lachlan.

I started to walk over to the car, when I saw this man get out. All I could think was, *'Holy shit, he has a beard'*. I was used to seeing a baby-faced young man, but Lachlan actually had facial hair now, it was really sexy. I couldn't wipe the smile from my face once we locked eyes. I walked over to Lachlan, he kissed me on the cheek and gave me a cuddle. He smelt amazing!! Lachlan did the gentlemanly thing and helped me with my bag, and even opened the car door for me, which was something I definitely wasn't used to.

On the drive back to Lachlan's house, we talked as if we had known each other all of our lives. We sang and laughed together, then Lachlan put his hand on my leg. I freaked out, not because I was scared, but because it had been a long time since anyone had touched me. Thank god I shaved above the knee, or I think he would have turned the car around and dropped me back off to the airport. When we were pulling up in the drive way, I kept saying to myself, *'Take it easy with him, DO NOT HAVE SEX WITH HIM'*.

As soon as we were inside, he scooped me up. I wrapped my legs around his waist, we kissed and somehow made it to his bedroom in about two seconds flat. I don't even know why I bothered trying to tell myself that I wouldn't have sex with Lachlan. The attraction I felt for this man was like nothing I had ever felt. The sex that day was the most amazing sex I had ever had. I always felt like sex was a chore, or I had to be drunk to do it, but Lachlan and I had an electricity that I can't even describe. We even cuddled after sex, which was also very rare for me. We laid in bed, cuddling and talking, which also shocked me because my affection levels were never high either. I had never felt safer in my life.

Although Lachlan and I were having a great time together, I was so afraid. I didn't know what to expect from him, I didn't know what he wanted from me and I was too scared to ask.

The next day, he took me out for lunch and showed me some lovely parts of Perth, and as we arrived back to his house, he told me that he was falling for me. I was petrified now, not because he said what he did, but because I was, once again, about to rush into another relationship and it would end up a mess. I couldn't just stand back and not say I felt the same, because I would be lying to him and to myself. Once we decided that we both really liked each other, it was time to get back on a plane and go home. I didn't want to go but I missed

Hudson so much. Lachlan mentioned something about me going home and forgetting about him, which I knew wasn't going to happen. I told him that I wanted to be his girlfriend. The smile on that man's face was enormous and so adorable. He accepted what I said and that was that, we were now a couple.

Saying goodbye at the airport was sad. I wanted Lachlan to come with me and he wanted me to stay, but I got on the plane and went home. We spoke on the phone all the time after my visit, but the more we spoke, the more I missed him. I was thinking about returning to Perth again, but with Hudson this time. Lachlan wasn't due to be back in Darwin until March, it was the very start of February, and I just couldn't handle not seeing Lachlan for another month. So once again, I got on the internet and booked flights to Perth, with Hudson this time. I knew that by bringing Hudson, Lachlan could see me as a mother as well as a partner and him getting to know Hudson was very important to me, because if he didn't like Hudson in any way, I knew it just wasn't meant to be.

My dad ended picked Hudson and I up from the airport in Perth. Dad was very accepting of Lachlan and I, he had only briefly met him when I visited last time and he was happy for me. His words to me in the car on the way to Lachlan's were, *'As long as he doesn't turn out like that dickhead ex of yours, then I'm happy'*. I had a bit of a giggle and I reassured Dad that Lachlan was nothing like Tom.

When we arrived at Lachlan's house, I got out of the car with Hudson and knocked on the door. Lachlan answered the door, grabbed Hudson and gave him a cuddle. Lachlan was happy to see us, I think he was missing me just as much as I was missing him.

Hudson and I spent four weeks in Perth. Lachlan went to work during the week, and would spend the weekends with us, either hanging out at his place or exploring Perth. One afternoon when Lachlan was dancing around the lounge room with Hudson, Hudson called him 'Dad'.

I looked over awkwardly at Lachlan and said, *'You definitely don't have to answer to that, I would never expect you to'*.

Lachlan was fine with being called Dad. I was the one freaking out about it, I didn't want Lachlan thinking that he had to be called Dad.

After Hudson dropped the Dad bomb, Lachlan and I started talking about babies. He eventually wanted children, in fact he had names picked out, which I was eager to hear. He didn't have any girls names, only boys, which clearly meant he wanted a son. He said the first name, Angus, the second name was Zayn, which was quickly removed when I told him that was the name of a band member from One Direction, then he said a name I had never heard before. He said the name 'Bryson'. I absolutely loved it, I pulled out my phone and wrote

Bryson in my notes. I didn't want to forget that name, it was really beautiful.

Hudson and I had so much fun in Perth but it was time to go. Lachlan wouldn't be far behind us anyway, he was going to drive to Darwin in a week or so, which went by so fast. It felt like I blinked and Lachlan was almost in Darwin. I could hardly wait to see him. I drove down to the supermarket to grab some milk and bread, checked my phone on the way out and saw a missed call from Lachlan. I figured I would call him back when I got home, but as I was pulling into my driveway, Lachlan was standing there waiting for me. I have never stopped my car so fast before, I threw my seat belt off, opened the car door and gave Lachlan a huge cuddle and kiss. I was ecstatic knowing that he was back home with Hudson and I.

I took him inside to meet my mum and Mike. Hudson was playing in the lounge room when he spotted Lachlan, and his little face lit up. Lachlan scooped Hudson up and kissed him on the cheek. I told Lachlan to drop his gear off into my room, and that I would help him unpack. As we walked into the bedroom, I shut the door and locked it. Lachlan and I had about ten minutes to spare so we took advantage of that time. We didn't use protection, which worried me.

I said later that afternoon that I was going to make a doctor's appointment as soon as I got my next period and ask about contraception. Neither of us were ready for a child together, so I wanted to do the right thing before I fell pregnant. A couple of weeks after Lachlan arrived home, I started to feel sick when I was running the stairs at the esplanade. I only did ten laps then went home – I thought maybe the heat was too much for me that day. Lachlan and I had also booked in for a tattoo, which was maybe a week after I felt sick whilst exercising. The whole time I was being tattooed I wanted to faint. I was sweating and feeling like I was going to hit the deck at any moment. A quick thought flashed through my mind about being pregnant, but I didn't say anything to Lachlan because I thought maybe I could be wrong. Instead I waited until the day I was due for my period. If I didn't have it by lunchtime on the day I was due, I knew I was going to be pregnant.

My period due date had arrived, I patiently waited for it to happen, but by lunch time, there was no sign of it. I pulled Lachlan aside to tell him that we needed to go get a pregnancy test. Lachlan couldn't understand why, he figured I would get it later that day or maybe even the next day, but I knew my body and I knew it wasn't coming at all. We ended up at the chemist at around 1:30pm. I bought two tests. We went back to the house, I peed into a disposable cup, dipped the test in, and left it on the bathroom sink. I went into the kitchen to do the dishes. Lachlan was sitting outside on the phone – I could see how relaxed he looked. He didn't have a worry in the world, but after 60 seconds of endless butterflies in my tummy, I went to check the test. When I picked it up and saw the positive sign, I started to shake. As I came out of the bathroom, I could see Lachlan was off the phone.

I opened the back door and said, *'Well, you're going to be a dad'*.

I expected him to be so upset, but he got out if his seat, walked over to me, picked me up, spun me around and said, *'I'm so fucking happy right now'*.

I couldn't believe it; I was pregnant after dating Lachlan for two months. I was happy to be having a baby, but I was so afraid that this pregnancy could potentially destroy us.

If only I knew how right I was going to be.

Chapter 8

There's no heartbeat

Telling my friends and family about the pregnancy was easy. Although a lot of people were in shock, they were still very happy for me. Lachlan wasn't sure about telling his mother and sister yet, which made me feel like they weren't going to be happy at all. Every time I suggested that Lachlan tell his family, he said he wasn't ready. I knew he was anxious to call them and break the news but he had to tell them at some point, so he decided to call his sister, Ruth, and tell her first. We were driving into town at the time of the call, so I was able to hear the entire conversation through the car. When Ruth answered the phone, Lachlan said, *'You're going to be an aunty'*.

Ruth instantly started saying, *'Oh no Lachie, no, no'*. It was the most awkward thing to hear, because Ruth didn't get the chance to even know I was in the car yet. The second Ruth didn't show Lachlan any support, he hung up on her.

I sat quietly, not really knowing what to say. Because Lachlan and I were excited, I just assumed his family would be as well. Five minutes later, Ruth called back and apologised. She said how worried she was that Lachlan had knocked up an 18-year-old.

He started to laugh, *'Jasmin is 28, not 18'*.

Ruth was quick to accept the pregnancy once she knew I was actually older than her. She found out that I was in the car and apologised for coming across as a bitch. I didn't know Ruth, but I could tell she felt like an absolute ass and her apology was genuine. She mentioned that she would come and visit in a couple of months, so she could get to know me a little better, which I was excited for.

The next phone call was to Lachlan's mother, Ethel. I wasn't around for the call but Lachlan said she took the news really well, which I was a little shocked about because Lachlan was so scared to tell her. At least that part was out of the way and we could go ahead and tell everyone else about our bundle of joy, who was due on November 29th.

There's no heartbeat

I went to my very first antenatal appointment when I was around 16 weeks. I sat and spoke to a doctor to talk about my birthing plan. The doctor had said that I was allowed to have another C-section if I wanted to, or to try my luck at a VBAC (vaginal birth after caesarean). I liked that I was allowed to have a choice, because it was my body after all, so I should get the choice. After seeing the doctor, I saw a midwife. I was handed a bag of stuff to read about pregnancy, miscarriage, breastfeeding and postnatal depression, but the best part was that I got to hear the baby's heartbeat. I always loved the sound of a baby's heartbeat, especially when it came to my own children.

After my appointment was finished, I met up with Simone and we had some lunch together, then I asked her a very important question. I asked her to be in the delivery room with Lachlan and I when I had the baby, if I had a VBAC. Simone of course said she would. She was my sister after all, so if I was going to have a natural delivery, I wanted both her and Lachlan there to hold my hand. Lachlan and I had already spoken about it, and he was fine with Simone being there for not only me but him too.

Our 20-week scan was in a couple of days, which usually I would be so excited for because that's when you can find out the baby's gender, but Lachlan and I had agreed on keeping the gender a surprise. We both didn't want another baby after this little one was born, so we figured it would be a special way to find out the gender. When I was having my ultrasound, the sonographer was so cheeky, he kept saying, *'I know what you're having'*. I almost said, *'Just bloody tell us,'* but I stayed strong and so did Lachlan. The sonographer asked if I had any morning sickness.

'Hell yes, I do,' I said.

I was throwing up every night around 7pm. It would only go for a couple of hours but it drained the hell out of me, especially when I worked an afternoon shift at the supermarket. My ultrasound looked really good, the baby was healthy which is always lovely to hear. We were given a disk of photos to take home and keep, but the sonographer made sure not to load any gender reveal pictures onto the disk. I think he knew I would sneak a peek if I had the chance.

It wasn't long after my ultrasound that Ruth came to visit Lachlan and I. She was softly spoken and really nice. She would tell me about Lachlan being a pain in the ass when he was a kid, which didn't surprise me. We explored Darwin together, talked a lot about Ethel, and Ruth warned me that Ethel can come across as a bitch. I had dealt with bitches before, so I didn't feel like that was anything to worry about. Ruth only stayed for four days then she had to leave. I was sad as she was so easy to get along with, and it was nice to have another woman in the house for a while. Ruth mentioned coming back once the baby was born.

'We will let you know as soon as I'm in labour,' I promised her.

Over the next few weeks, I had a lovely daily routine at home. Hudson would have a sleep at 12pm, I would pour myself a glass of water with a lime, grab some snacks and scroll through Ebay, whilst watching 'One Born Every Minute'. I was obsessed with the show. I loved seeing all the beautiful, healthy babies being born into the arms of doting parents. One of the episodes that came on wasn't so joyful. A mother had given birth to a stillborn baby. I watched in horror as this tiny little baby was born. The pain on the mother's face was enough to make me bawl like a baby, I was an absolute mess watching it. The mother was interviewed a few weeks after her birth and I remember seeing how strong she was on camera. She was saying that her baby was now in a better place, due to it having so many complications in the womb. That woman was instantly my hero, the way she carried herself throughout the interview was so brave.

After seeing that episode, I stayed away from One Born for a couple of weeks, but Lachlan was interested in the show and what it was all about, so I brought up an episode on YouTube for us to watch, and I'll be damned, it was another episode of a woman who had to give birth to her dead baby. Lachlan and I discussed the episode once it had finished. We both said very similar things; we said that we would just die if we went through that.

There was no way, as a mother, that I could ever get through losing a child. Lachlan reassured me that our baby wouldn't die.

'This baby is a Hill baby, and Hill babies don't die,' he said as he puffed his chest out and put his hands on his hips just like superman.

Lachlan always made an awkward or sad time funny. I loved that about him, and I was going to miss it as he was going away for five weeks for work. I didn't know how I was going to survive without him. He had been cooking for me most nights.

'2-minute noodles, it is,' I joked.

Hudson and I dropped Lachlan off to the airport and said goodbye. Hudson was very close to Lachlan now, so he found it hard to say goodbye. It felt like Lachlan was gone five minutes when I started to get a cold. It wasn't anything major, I could continue to do my daily chores and look after Hudson. Then a week went by. I had the flu pretty bad, so I took myself to the doctor. The doctor told me there was nothing he could give me due to my pregnancy and to just go home and rest. Thankfully Hudson was a well-behaved almost-two-year-old. I would lay on the couch while he would build block houses or read stories to me. He made it so much easier to rest.

There's no heartbeat

It was around week three of being sick, and by this stage I was coughing all day and all night. I would sit up to sleep, and I was coughing so hard, I started to bleed. I rang the maternity ward straight away to let them know, but their advice was to just take cough medicine and rest. I had blood come out of my vagina whilst pregnant and they didn't ask me to go in for a check-up? I found that strange. Thankfully the bleeding only happened that once and never again.

I ended up going to see a different doctor for a second opinion about my cough. After checking my breathing, the doctor let me know that I had pneumonia, which explained why I was coughing so much. I was put straight on antibiotics. I called Lachlan to tell him, he offered to fly home, but I couldn't do that to him. I had survived this long being sick on my own, I could last another two weeks without him. Once I started feeling better, I decided to google photographers in Darwin for a maternity photo shoot, and I ended up finding a girl who was holding a competition. Two families would win a free maternity photoshoot with her, all we had to do was enter and she would randomly choose the winners. I entered, not even thinking I would win. I wasn't the type to win stuff like that, so later that day when she posted my name as one of the winners on her social media page, I was blown away. I was so excited, the shoot would happen just after Lachlan got back, which was perfect.

Finally Lachlan returned from his work trip, and he couldn't believe how much my belly had popped. Hudson hogged him the first four hours he was home; I didn't mind though, it was good seeing them bond the way they did.

'My mum is coming to visit in a week,' Lachlan told me.

I wouldn't say I was excited to meet her, but I was glad to be getting it out of the way. When we first met, I got that feeling instantly that she didn't approve of me, it was this look in her eye. I could just see that she was judging everything about me. She brought along her partner, Ron. Ron seemed ok; he was nice to Hudson which is always a bonus in my book. Speaking to Ethel, I could tell that she had money. She wore such lovely clothes, and little old me bought my clothes from the second-hand shops, just so I could afford to spoil Hudson with gifts and new clothes.

Ethel and Ron were only in Darwin for a day when Lachlan and I had our maternity photoshoot. It was a really hot day that day. So hot, we decided to leave Hudson at home with my mum. Lachlan and I met the photographer about 40 minutes away from our place. The photographers name was Emma; she was young with two boys of her own, so we clicked instantly. I was wearing a big yellow tutu and a little white top, so I could show off my belly. Lachlan was in a t-shirt and shorts. We spent about half an hour getting some great pictures together as we were sweating half to death from the humidity. Right near the end of the photoshoot, Lachlan suggested that he would change into a nice shirt and jeans because he was feeling uncomfortable in such causal clothes. I found it a little weird that he wanted to put more layers on, but I understood that he wanted to look a little nicer for the photos. Emma was taking photos of me standing up, with Lachlan on the ground on one knee, kissing my belly. I was just about to ask if Lachlan was too hot in his clothes when he pulled a box out of his pocket. As he opened it up, I put my hands over my mouth in shock.

'Jasmin, will you marry me?' he asked, with the biggest smile on his face.

I began to cry tears of joy.

'Of course I will,' I replied.

Emma came over to congratulate us and to let Lachlan know that he did a great job of hiding the proposal. Turns out Lachlan had asked Emma to organise a surprise proposal photo. This was while I was in the bathroom wiping the Darwin sweat from my face.

Emma promised to get the pictures to us ASAP, and left. As Lachlan and I got in the car to go home, I called Simone to tell her the news. As usual we had a little squeal together. Simone congratulated Lachlan and I, and I asked her to be my maid of honour, to which Simone happily agreed.

I texted Mum to let her know the news, and she was just as happy for Lachlan and I. I felt so lucky to have such a decent man in my life and the fact that he wanted to marry me, that was just a bonus. Lachlan mentioned telling his mum when we got back to our place. *'Shit, I forgot about Ethel,'* I thought. I was afraid that she wouldn't accept it. Lachlan told me that Ethel liked me and I had nothing to worry about. So when we got back to our place and saw Ethel and Ron were there, I began to panic. We walked inside and I went straight upstairs to change. I was hoping Lachlan would tell Ron and Ethel whilst I was changing, but he waited until I came back downstairs. When Lachlan announced the news, Ethel didn't say a lot, she cuddled Lachlan and said *'Congratulations'* – meanwhile I was standing there like an idiot, thinking, *'Yep, she hates me'.*

Ron ended up saying congratulations to me, which eased my mind a little bit, but it was such an awkward situation, I was so relieved when they left to go out for dinner. The following morning, Ethel and Ron invited us for coffee before they flew back to Adelaide. I figured this could be my way of trying to get Ethel's approval of me, which I hate admitting because her opinion shouldn't have mattered, but I really loved Lachlan and didn't want his mum making things really awkward between us. As we sat and drank our coffee, I just couldn't think of much to say. I sat there like a stunned mullet for a good 15 minutes, until Ron asked me about baby names. Lachlan and I hadn't really discussed girl names, but Bryson was definitely his name if it was a boy, and I knew deep down I was having a boy (mother's instinct really is a magical thing). Lachlan had said that he wanted to name the baby Bryson, but Ethel hated the name. Lachlan suggested Montgomery, which I was definitely saying 'No' to! Ethel hated that name too but Lachlan, being the sarcastic human that he is, made Ethel believe that was what he was going to call our son.

When it was time to say goodbye to Ethel and Ron, Lachlan gave his mum a big hug. She cried, which was actually nice to see. You could see she was going to miss her boy. Over the next few days, I was feeling more and more uncomfortable. It was late October, I had roughly five weeks to go and I was feeling pissed off every second of the damn day. I found it harder to nap during the day, so when Hudson would go for his sleep, I would sit on our spare couch in the kitchen and listen to music. As I sat there feeling like I was a beached whale, I began to doze off. I remember the song that was playing as I was dozing off, it was 'Fix You' by Coldplay. I wasn't in a deep sleep because I could still hear the music playing but I started to dream. I dreamt that I was walking in front of a tiny coffin, small enough for a baby to fit inside. The coffin was pink, and I looked behind me to see Lachlan carrying the coffin. It was the weirdest feeling, it was like I was awake, watching my life flash before my eyes. I was soon woken up by Hudson crying, so I went and got him out of his cot, still shaking from my dream. I held Hudson in my arms and called Lachlan to tell him about my dream. Lachlan was so good at calming me down in shitty situations, he told me not to worry, it was just a dream and my hormones were all over the place. I calmed down, stopped shaking but I did say, *'Tomorrow at my midwife appointment, I am requesting a C section'*.

As much as I felt calm, something deep inside of me didn't feel quite right. The next morning I arrived at my midwife appointment, and in the waiting room sat roughly eight pissed off pregnant women. The midwives were really behind with their appointments that day. I sat down, grabbed a magazine and slowly made my way through it to pass the time. I heard my name being called from down the hall. The midwife was calling me before she arrived to the waiting room, so she was definitely in a rush. As we walked to the room, she introduced herself as Carol. I was polite and said, *'Nice to meet you'*.

We made it to the room, sat down and before we could start the appointment, another midwife came in and told Carol she had ten minutes, then just walked out. It was strange but we just carried on with our appointment. The baby was measured, I heard the heartbeat, she asked if I had any more children, it was a nice conversation and everything seemed normal. Carol asked if I had any concerns. That's when I told her I wanted to book in for a C-section. Carol dropped her pen on the desk, looked me dead in the eye and said, *'How are you going to look after a toddler if you have a C-section?'*

She then went on to ask if I have stairs in my house.

'Yes,' I responded, very confused.

'How will you climb stairs in your house with a newborn, if you want a C-section?'

I couldn't even answer her questions properly because the same midwife kept walking in and telling Carol to wrap it up. By this stage I just felt like a number, not a human. I also felt like Carol was a bit of a bitch. I was made to feel guilty for wanting a C-section, even though I was told I could choose either. I ended up telling Carol about my dream and that I would feel a lot better if the baby was born at 38 weeks, via a C-section.

Carol just didn't want to hear about anything I had to say, she was all for a VBAC. I ended up agreeing with her.

'Maybe a C-section is a silly choice. You are the expert after all,' I said to Carol.

She was happy I went with the VBAC, signed my paperwork and shuffled me out of the room. Once again, I was on the phone crying to poor Lachlan. I felt as though she forced me to go through with a VBAC, I felt mistreated and like my choices didn't matter. One good thing was that Simone could also be there when I gave birth, so that gave me some hope.

The following day I went to a wedding expo with Simone. She was looking forward to picking out things for her wedding. I was just proud to come along with her as bridesmaid duty. We strolled around the expo, looking at every single stall. Simone was getting some great ideas for her wedding, and I had found a cupcake stand which had free cupcakes to try, so we were both in our element.

November 1st 2015, Lachlan, Hudson and I were at the local shopping centre. We had a trolley full of last minute baby things to put into the hospital bag, and as we were leaving the store, Hudson was having a major melt down. He wanted to sit on Lachlan's shoulders whilst we were going down the travelator. I was becoming slightly embarrassed by Hudson's behaviour, so I took the trolley and allowed him to hop onto Lachlan's shoulders. As I pushed the trolley onto the travelator, a lady stood behind me very closely with her trolley. As we got to the bottom, I went to push the trolley off the end, but the wheels of the trolley got stuck on the bottom of the guard. I was stuck. I was trying hard to push my trolley off, but the lady's trolley behind me was crushing my belly between my trolley and hers. Lachlan was hanging onto Hudson by one hand and trying to rip the trolley away from my stomach.

'You're being crushed babe,' Lachlan yelled.

I looked down and my trolley was crushing my stomach, while the trolley behind me was crushing my back, There were a heap of people in the eatery watching, probably not thinking much of what was happening, until I looked over at Lachlan to see him running off the travelator away from me. I couldn't see Hudson with him. I instantly knew then that Hudson had fallen off the travelator, which was a four-metre drop. I don't know how it happened but I managed to rip the trolley out from my stomach. I ran to the edge of the travelator where Hudson had fallen, I was screaming, *'Please someone save my baby'*.

People came from every angle of the shopping centre after I screamed for help. A lovely young girl got me a chair and cuddled me as I sobbed, waiting to be told my son was dead. There was no way he would have survived that fall. I could see Lachlan walking back towards me with Hudson in his arms. Hudson wasn't moving, and he had blood trickling from his mouth. A man beat Lachlan back to me and had told me that Hudson was ok but was in shock. Hudson had actually fallen off the travelator, hit another travelator on the way down and when he landed, someone scooped him up and helped him before Lachlan arrived. By now there was security everywhere, and they started to shuffle me away, but I wouldn't leave without Hudson and Lachlan. I waited for them to be right by my side so we could leave together. The ambulance arrived; I was begging them to tell me if he was going to be ok, but they couldn't give me an answer yet.

On the way to the hospital, Hudson was laying on Lachlan. He was still so silent. Lachlan was trying to remain calm but I could see that he was feeling guilty.

'This isn't your fault Lachlan; it was an accident,' I said as I rubbed his arm. Lachlan started to cry.

'What if the baby is hurt?' he asked.

I had been so worried about Hudson that I had forgotten all about the baby. The ambulance officer said I would be monitored once we arrived.

When we did arrive, there were doctors everywhere waiting for Hudson. We were wheeled into two different rooms, but I could still see Hudson and Lachlan. Mum and Mike showed up just after we arrived – I had texted them to get to the hospital. Mum thought I was in labour; I wish that's what it was.

The doctors took Hudson into another room, where they hooked him up to a heart monitor and checked his blood pressure. We were told that he possibly had broken hips, and internal bleeding.

I went in to see Hudson who was sleeping peacefully, the morphine that was pumped into him was obviously doing its job. I went to give him a kiss, but I accidentally woke him up. He slowly opened his eyes and said *'Dad'*.

'Do you want me to get Dad for you?' I asked, as I stroked his hair.

He nodded and said *'Dad'*. I called Lachlan into the room.

'He just wants you,' I said. *'Even he knows this isn't your fault, Lachlan.'* While Lachlan was sitting with Hudson, I had to go to the birthing suite so that the baby could be monitored for four hours. I had called Simone and told her what happened. She was by my side in a heartbeat, with a block of chocolate, and she stayed by my side the whole time. I appreciated that more than she knew.

Once the baby was given the all clear, I was able to go see Hudson. The doctors had run a heap of tests and found out that after Hudson falling four metres from a travelator, he only had a bruised liver. Lachlan and I couldn't believe it, the doctors kept calling Hudson 'The miracle child'.

Hudson and Lachlan spent the night in hospital, and I went home. I had a sleepless night. I was tossing and turning, I kept going into the nursery which wasn't set up yet, even though Lachlan was meant to do it three weeks ago, but I wasn't about to get all huffy about that. I was just so thankful that Hudson and the baby were ok, so I decided to pack my hospital bag. I was packing all necessary items you need when you have a baby, and when it came time to pack the baby's clothing, I knew I wouldn't need anything pink. Everything I packed was for a boy, except for one pink item. I only packed it just in case my mothers instinct was way out of whack and a girl did end up being born.

The next few weeks flew by, and before we knew it, it was our baby's due date. I had been getting Braxton Hicks a lot and had been to the hospital so many times during the weeks prior, only to be sent home with sleeping pills every time. I was feeling like the baby would never come. I was sitting on the couch in the lounge room, when all of a sudden, the baby started kicking really fast. I told Lachlan to come and feel the baby moving.

'This could be the last time you feel him move, so lap it up,' I said.

We both had our hands on my belly feeling the baby wriggle around. I looked at Lachlan, we were both smiling at each other and that's when I realised, I was 100% happy with my life. I let all those walls down with Lachlan, the ones I never let down with Anna or Tom. I was genuinely in love and couldn't wait to have Lachlan's baby. I especially looked forward to breastfeeding properly this time around.

Just before we went to bed, I looked at Lachlan and said, *'I love you so much Lachlan and I can't wait to have this baby with you, you will be the best Dad'*.

Lachlan smiled and said, *'Thank you honey, I love you too'*. It was a really special moment.

The next chapter of our lives was going to be amazing; I just knew it.

The next day I woke up feeling like today was the day, I was going to have a baby.

I called Lachlan, who was at work, to come and pick me up. He pulled into the driveway singing at the top of his lungs, *'I'M GOING TO BE A DAD'*. I shook my head laughing. It was great seeing Lachlan so excited. He threw the nappy bag in the car and as I was about to get in, he asked if he could have a quick shower. A few choice words came from my mouth after he asked that. After he explained that he wanted to wear his favourite top for the very first photos with his baby, who could say no to that? I quickly texted Simone and told her to be on standby.

Arriving at the hospital felt weird. We had been there so many times the past week and it was so quiet, but today was really busy, there were women having babies everywhere. We were asked to wait in the waiting area until a room was free. As we were waiting, I started to get a slight contraction, and I thought to myself, *'This baby will be born today without a doubt'*. Once a room was all cleaned up, we were able to go in and wait for a midwife. The midwife we saw was one who had been there most of the time when we were there thinking I was in labour; her name was Annie and I didn't like her. I felt like she thought we were that annoying couple who came in when they really shouldn't.

Annie started to search for the baby's heartbeat with the doppler. She didn't have much luck but she had said that the last lady who came in had the same issue with that doppler and they ended up finding a heartbeat, so Annie went and grabbed a different doppler. Lachlan asked If I had felt the baby move at all today.

'Of course I have,' I said.

Then I started to wonder if I actually had felt the baby move. I began to poke on my belly to see if that would get the baby to wriggle, but nothing happened. Lachlan was becoming very worried but I was fine, I felt like everything would be ok.

Annie returned and started to try to locate the baby's heartbeat, but again, she found nothing. She suggested bringing a doctor in with an ultrasound machine, that way we could see the baby and make sure everything was ok.

By this stage, Lachlan was white in the face. I was a little panicked but I still felt like maybe both dopplers were just not doing their job properly. A doctor returned with the ultrasound machine, and as soon as she started to search for the baby's heartbeat, I looked straight at Lachlan. I knew his face would give me the answer of whether it was bad or good news. It only took roughly 20 seconds, then Lachlan's face dropped. I quickly looked over at the doctor who was looking very concerned.

She turned to me and said, *'I'm so sorry, but there's no heartbeat'*. The tears instantly fell from my eyes. Lachlan grabbed me and held me whilst we cried together. I looked over at Annie who had a look of disbelief on her face.

She kept saying, *'But I have seen you both so many times this week and everything was fine'*. Annie was definitely in just as much shock as Lachlan I both were.

Lachlan ended up losing it, he was throwing chairs and punching the wall. I really had to just forget that our baby was gone for a second and calm him down. I was hugging him, whispering, *'Everything will be ok'*. Eventually he settled, then we had the task of telling our close family that the baby had died. Lachlan offered to call Mum; I just didn't want to tell her. Mum said she would have Hudson at her place for as long as we needed.

I ended up calling my dad. When he answered he said, *'Jesus you sound like you're in pain, are you having the baby?'*

'Sorry Dad, the baby died,' I said as I was fighting back tears.

Dad was screaming down the phone, he kept saying, *'No, no, no'*. It broke my heart.

He suggested I call Shalanda. If anyone knew what it was like to lose a baby, my sister would know. I didn't want to bother her though – she was having her own personal troubles, so I called Rikki-Lee instead. Rikki was speechless, I was fucking speechless. Rikki said she would pass the news onto Shalanda. I received a text five minutes later from Shalanda. She was heartbroken for us. I didn't even have the heart to tell Simone. She was meant to be in the room with me while I had the baby, I had let her down. Lachlan called her and broke the news to her and once again, my best friend raced to be by my side. As Simone walked in the doors of the birthing room, we both just burst into tears. She cuddled me so tight.

Lachlan went downstairs to call his mother and sister. I sat on the bed saying, *'Why has this happened?'* I just didn't understand how? What about Hudson? How am I going to tell him? My mind was racing a thousand miles an hour with questions. Once Lachlan returned, two doctors and two midwives popped in to have a chat. They wanted me to be induced straight away. I instantly said, *'No way'*. I wanted a C-section at 38 weeks, my son was now dead, so they could give me my C-section.

The doctors recommended VBAC otherwise there would be a risk of infection, but I was not going to be induced.

I knew I wouldn't be able to birth my dead child, I just knew I wasn't strong enough.

One of the doctors, Katy, had informed me that they couldn't give me a C-section that day because it wasn't an emergency. They were fully booked the next day as well, so we were sent home for two days, where we waited to give birth to our baby. I kept thinking I could feel movements, I was sure the baby was kicking. I called the hospital and told Katy, but Katy told me that because the baby was deceased, it would be just floating around in my womb, which was making me feel like there was movements.

The morning I was scheduled for the C-section, I was up at 4am. I kept thinking that if the baby was a boy, Lachlan would be devastated – I knew how much he wanted a son. As much as it would hurt no matter what the gender was, I hoped for a girl. I thought if it were a girl, Lachlan wouldn't hurt as much. At 5am I had a shower and looked in the mirror at my belly one last time.

'I will miss you,' I said, as I rubbed my beautiful bump.

Simone had texted me to say she couldn't be at the hospital while I had Bryson. All our plans and talking about her being there when my baby was born were thrown out the window.

Lachlan grabbed my hand and said, *'It's time to go now'*.

I sobbed as he walked me out to the car. I didn't know how the hell I was going to do this, I didn't want to do this, but I knew I didn't have a choice.

CHAPTER 9

Dear Bryson

Dear Bryson,

On the 2nd December 2015, I arrived at the hospital to give birth to you. I still didn't know if you were a boy or a girl yet. All the nurses and midwives knew you were already gone, so they made sure they took great care of us while we waited for me to go in for a C-section. Your dad was trying to keep me smiling. Telling me jokes and making me laugh, which helped me a lot. The nurses came and wheeled me into a waiting room, your dad was right there with me. I remember so many different people introducing themselves to me, but I was crying so much I wasn't really taking notice of what they were all saying. I was shaking like a leaf. I didn't want to birth you and not take you home, this wasn't the plan. Your dad and I had talked about naming you

Hunter if you were a boy, we loved the name Bryson so much, but we couldn't bring ourselves to use it anymore. The doctors took me into a big cold room. It felt like a morgue, and it was where they were going to take you out of my stomach.

I saw Doctor Katy in the room, but I didn't recognise anyone else. I had your dad to the left of me holding my hand, and a lovely nurse to the right of me also holding my hand. My heart rate was really high. The doctors wanted to put me to sleep but I knew that your dad couldn't be there if I was asleep, so I stayed strong for both you and Dad. I took some big breaths and my heart rate slowed down. The doctors began my C-section. The nurse who was holding my hand was crying, she was so sad. I rubbed her hand and asked if she was ok. I didn't want her to cry. I was so nervous; my jaw and teeth were chattering so much that your dad couldn't really understand what I was saying. All of a sudden, I felt a familiar feeling, just like when your big brother was born. It felt like all of my organs were being ripped out, which meant you were almost ready to come out. I turned to your dad and said, 'The baby is almost here', but I don't think he understood me through my chattering teeth. I felt my whole body relax, which meant at 9:20am, you were born. I closed my eyes so tight, waiting and hoping for you to cry. I was thinking, 'Please cry, please'. Sadly, you never did. There was silence, not just from you but from everyone in the room.

Dad was asked if he wanted to go and meet you and to find out if you were a boy or a girl. He also cut your cord while he was meeting you. Your dad came back over to me, sat down, kissed me on the cheek and said, 'I knew it would be a boy'. My heart sank. Tears fell from my eyes. I had let your dad down. He asked if I wanted to meet you, I said 'Yes' but just as your dad was bringing you to me, I changed my mind. I was so afraid; I didn't know what I was going to see. Just as your dad went to put you back into your little hospital crib, I asked to hold you. I watched your dad bringing you over to me; you looked so beautiful all rugged up in a blanket. As Dad gently placed you into my arms, I was blown away with how much you looked like Hudson. You were just perfect. I was freezing cold at the time, but your warm little body started to keep me warm. I was amazed by your black hair with little curls near your ears, just like your dad gets. A midwife asked if your dad and I wanted to put Hunter on your little birth card, but we both knew you weren't a Hunter; you were Bryson, from the very beginning. Once I was ready to go to recovery, a nurse wheeled me into an elevator. I was holding you in my arms with Dad by our side. The nurse kept covering your little face while we were heading to recovery. I would uncover you and she would cover you right back up again. The nurse told me that you, an innocent little baby, could offend someone if they saw you. I told that nurse that I was damn proud of you and I was showing you off just like all the other mothers get to do when their children are born.

We were lucky enough to be given a cuddle cot for you to stay in, so that we could spend some time with you. We had some really beautiful photos taken with you, and a lovely lady came to meet you and made some little hand and feet moulds from you, so we had something to remember you by.

By the end of the day, you were so cold. I just wanted to wrap you up and cuddle you so you stayed warm, but I wasn't allowed to. We had to keep putting you back into the cuddle cot if you were being held too much.

The next day, you didn't look the same, your lips were going really red and the colour from your cheeks had disappeared, but you were still so beautiful. I picked you up to cuddle you good morning, when all of a sudden, your nose started to bleed. I panicked, so I put you back in your cot. After that, I didn't hold you as much, unless your dad passed you to me because he had mastered how to pick you up without blood coming out of your nose. I kept looking over at the fully packed hospital bag in the corner, which was now full of blankets that you were wrapped in when you were first born. I wanted to take an outfit from the bag and dress you, but I knew by doing that I would become more attached to you, which I didn't want to do, because you were leaving the next day.

So many flowers were delivered to us while we were in hospital. Our room looked like a florist and they were all for you my baby boy. Some people even got to meet you, and were lucky enough to cuddle you. I didn't allow for your big brother to meet you; he wasn't even two yet and I felt the need to protect him from the death of you. I did want Simone to meet you though. She would have spoiled you, but Simone was afraid, she was scared of death. It hurt that she didn't want to see you but I understood.

Once day two was over, I went to sleep very quickly. I was exhausted. At around 2am I woke up to a baby crying, I thought it was you crying. I got out of bed, walked out into the hall way and started to search for you. As I woke up properly, I realised it was someone else's baby. Someone's baby that was alive. I sat in a chair in the hallway, with my head down, hiding my tears. A nurse approached me, knowing that I was your mum. She gave me something to help me sleep and sent me back to bed.

By day 3, I just couldn't look at you anymore, you had started to decompose. I didn't want you to leave me but I couldn't bear to see you like that anymore. Dad and I arranged for you to go to the morgue at 6pm, which meant we got to spend the rest of the day saying goodbye. Doctor Katy came to see us, she was finishing for the day and knew it was my last day with you, so she was coming to say goodbye to you. I broke down after Doctor Katy asked how I felt about you leaving. I told her I wasn't ready to let you go. Katy cuddled me so tight as we both cried together. It was hard to think that once you left, you wouldn't come back. I pulled myself together. Katy waved goodbye to you and off she went.

Dad and I received a text from Simone an hour before you were due to leave. She had asked if it was ok to meet you, which made me very happy. Simone was able to visit you, cuddle you and get photos with you, I was so proud of her for putting aside her own fears just so she could say 'hello' and 'goodbye' to you.

I was watching the clock like a hawk the whole time Simone was visiting, and at exactly 6pm, a nurse knocked on the door. It was time for you to go now. Your dad handed you to me for one last big cuddle, I rubbed my nose against yours, told you that I loved you and I was going to miss you. I didn't cry as you left, I wanted to show you how strong I was. Dad was able to walk you to the morgue, he wanted to make sure you got there safely. As you were being pushed out in your little crib, I said, 'Bye baby, I love you,' and then you were gone. Simone was still visiting, she cuddled me and we cried together, knowing that was the very last time we would ever see you again.

Dad came back in tears, he didn't want you to go, he wanted you to stay forever. The nurse who returned with Dad was fighting back tears as well, she was telling us how strong we were, and that you were so beautiful. It was strange sleeping that night, knowing you weren't right beside us, we missed you so much already.

The following day we had to leave the hospital. I didn't want to, knowing you were still there. I wanted to stay until you were sent to Adelaide for an autopsy, but I knew I couldn't do that, so we packed our stuff and waited for a nurse to say we could go. We waited about an hour, when a young nurse walked in with a bag of drugs. She tossed them to me and said, 'Here's your bag of fun,' then left. I guess your death wasn't being taken seriously by some people.

As soon as we were discharged, your dad wheeled me out to the car. I still didn't have the energy to walk. I had an arm full of dead flowers, and no baby. I felt sad because I really wanted to know what colour your eyes were, but I was never game enough to open them. I mentioned to your dad that I will never know the colour of your eyes, but it turns out he had a sneak peek at them the day before you left us. Your eyes were a light blue, like Dad's. I really wanted you to have your dad's blue eyes – actually I wanted you to have everything of your dad's. I just forgot to say that I wanted you to have a heartbeat too.

When we were driving away from the hospital, I made your dad drive towards the building where the morgue was. He pointed to the door that you both went through the night before. I sat there, staring at the door, wishing it wasn't you who had to be taken through there. I blew you a kiss, your dad held my hand and we slowly drove away, I looked back at the morgue for as long as I could, before it disappeared. We drove home in silence with an empty car seat in the back. The hardest thing your dad and I had to do over those past few days, was to leave you behind. The thought of you being alone made us so sad. The only comfort we got was that when we left, we left you a huge piece of our hearts.

We miss you darling boy.

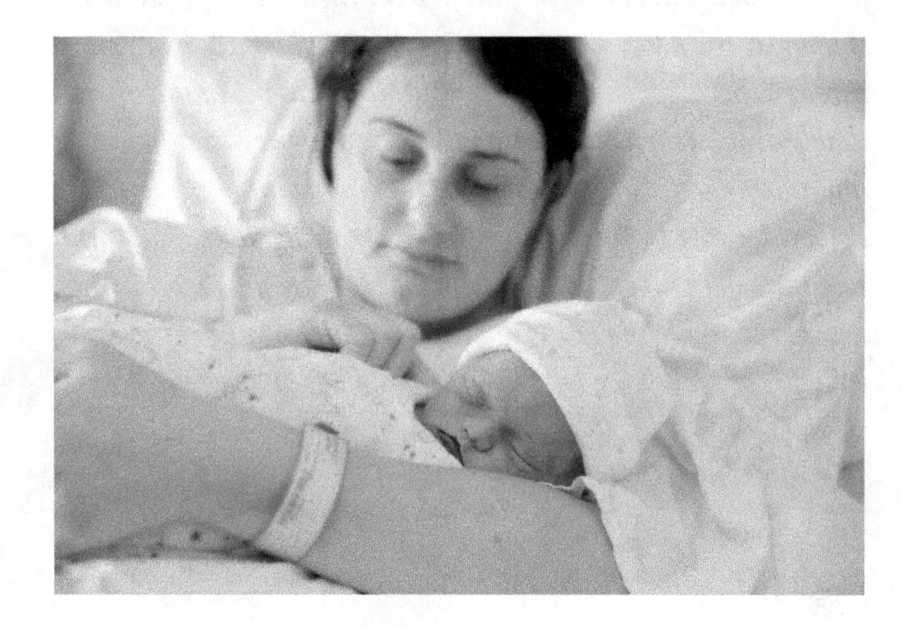

The Beauty in Bereavement

Dear Bryson

The Beauty in Bereavement

Dear Bryson

I wish you were here.

We Love you

Love Hudson and Lincoln

Chapter 10

The tipping point

After a very tearful drive home, Lachlan and I made our way upstairs to lay down.

I glanced over at the room which should have been Bryson's nursery. I walked in, looking around at everything that hadn't been unpacked yet like Bryson's bassinet, his clothes and toys. Lachlan put his hand on my shoulder. I remember being so annoyed that he never set up the nursery like he said he would, but now, I was grateful. There's no way I would have been able to come home to a beautifully set up nursery without my baby boy in my arms.

Later that night, Lachlan got a call from work. I was watching his body language and whatever was being said was making him feel very uncomfortable. He hung up the phone and told me he had to go back to work that Monday coming. I couldn't believe it, he had just lost his son, and was being made to go back to work. Apparently, he was needed.

'*But I need you too,*' I sobbed.

I didn't want him to leave me alone, it was too soon, but he was left with no choice. Monday came around and Lachlan went back to work. Hudson kept rubbing my belly and saying, '*Baby*', I would hold Hudson's hand and say, '*No darling, no more baby*'. What else could I say? He just wouldn't understand.

Mum was keeping me company while Lachlan worked. I spent all day sitting on the couch pumping my breasts as I had made the decision to donate my milk. I had found a lady on the internet who lived in Alice Springs who had breast cancer, and couldn't feed her newborn daughter. I had loads of milk, so I decided to donate it. I would cry as I pumped. I was looking forward to breastfeeding Bryson, and here I was doing a truly beautiful thing for someone, yet hating every second of it.

Four days after Bryson's little body was sent off for an autopsy, I received a call from Lachlan to say he was back in Darwin, safe and sound. I was so relieved. I just wanted him to be in the same town as I was, I didn't want him so far away.

The tipping point

Ten minutes after that call, he called me again and said, *'Jasmin, don't get upset but Bryson isn't back in Darwin, the morgue made a mistake and now his body is missing'*.

Something switched inside of me that day, I began to scream down the phone to Lachlan. I demanded to know where my son was. I was furious. Turns out Bryson couldn't be found in the morgue in Adelaide either, so if he wasn't in the Adelaide morgue, or the Darwin morgue, where the hell was he? I ended up calling the morgue in Darwin. I was shaking with anger, and as soon as someone answered I said, *'Where the fuck is my son?'* The lady on the other end knew who I was straight away – she had been dealing with Lachlan only moments before. I was than informed that Bryson had been found. A random funeral home had collected him. We hadn't asked for any funeral home to take our son. As far as we knew he was being sent back to Darwin so we could have a funeral for him. The lady who was speaking to me from the morgue apologised for the mix up.

'This isn't fucking McDonalds and you forgot my fries, you lost my fucking son,' I yelled down the phone, then hung up.

Lachlan finished work early that day to be with me, which I was extremely grateful for.

We had a chat about having Bryson's funeral in Adelaide. His body was already there and most of our family and friends lived in South Australia so it would save them from travelling. Plus, I thought maybe if Lachlan was surrounded by some of his family, he would find a little bit of comfort. We also talked about the possibility of moving to Perth. We both felt it would be best if we just moved on from such a traumatic experience in a place we both loved so much.

Mum found a really nice funeral home to have Bryson's funeral in the Adelaide Hills. The funeral director, Rick, was really friendly and supportive of our needs for the funeral so we booked in with him. Rick then had to go and pick up Bryson from the other funeral home, and as soon as he had Bryson he called me straight away. I asked for a picture of Bryson, I needed to know it was him. After all the mix ups, I didn't want to be given the wrong baby. Rick agreed and sent me a photo. I opened the message and there was my baby. His face had been sliced open and stitched back up, he was all wrapped up in the blanket we chose for him in Darwin, and he still had his little beanie on too. He looked so peaceful. So beautiful. I just wanted to cuddle him one last time, but it was too late. He was being cremated before we would even arrive in Adelaide.

Organising Bryson's funeral felt so surreal and wrong. *'Why did my baby have to die? Why us? There are plenty of people out there that have babies and don't take care of them, but we are being punished, our fucking son was punished.'* These are just some of the things Lachlan and I would say during our time of picking songs to play during the funeral. People were being so kind to us, they were offering us home-cooked meals, offering to take Hudson for a few hours so Lachlan and I could rest and basically just wanting to be there for us. I had never had so much support in my life. I actually thought with the support I was being offered, I would get through the grief just as quickly as I had gotten through everything else in my life. I was going to bounce back from this and be ok. All I had to do was get the funeral out of the way, then I could start to move on from this horrible nightmare.

Lachlan and I had decided to hold Bryson's funeral on the 23rd December. That gave us time to organise flights and to also allow the infection from my C-section to settle. I had been lifting Hudson out of his cot and putting him into bed with us, that way I could make sure that he was breathing throughout the night. I was definitely not allowed after having major surgery, but I needed to know that my only living child wasn't going to die on me too.

Ethel offered to pay for Lachlan, Hudson's and my flights to Adelaide for the funeral, and had also offered for us to stay with her and Ron. I was starting to think that maybe Ethel wasn't so bad after all. She was being so kind, which Lachlan and I appreciated so much. Lachlan had her book flights for the day before the funeral, which worried me. I didn't want anything bad to happen and have us miss Bryson's funeral. I had a lot of frozen breast milk to take with me. We were supposed to have a ten-minute stopover in Alice Springs, which gave me enough time to drop off the breast milk to the beautiful family I was donating to.

The morning we were due to fly out, there was a storm brewing in Darwin. There was so much lightning, I was sure our flight would be cancelled, but we were able to fly with no issues. We landed in Alice Springs on time, and I spotted the family I was donating to straight away. I walked over to them with a big smile on my face. I was so happy to meet such a brave family and their little baby girl, Sophie, was absolutely beautiful. It was a shame we couldn't stay, but we had to board our next flight, so we said our goodbyes to little Sophie and rushed over to our gate. I glanced over at the departure screen for our flight and noticed it said 'delayed'. I took a deep breath, and started to tell myself that it's ok, it will only be delayed for 20 minutes or so. We went and sat in a little café to give Hudson some morning tea, when Lachlan spotted his work mate, Lisa, who was also heading to Adelaide.

Lisa introduced herself to me. She was travelling alone so we invited her to sit with us. After about an hour of us waiting, not knowing what was happening with our flight, a flight attendant notified us that the plane that was meant to take us to Adelaide had some electrical issues and another plane was being flown over from

Adelaide to pick up the passengers and take them back to Adelaide. By this stage, I was fuming. I was pacing around the airport, screaming, *'We are going to miss our fucking son's funeral'*. Lachlan went and spoke to some flight crew who were heading to Adelaide with a different airline. As they were about to board, Lachlan was begging them to let us on the flight, but it was full. The anger that was running through me was something like I had never felt before. I then started to place blame on Lachlan for not booking our flights two days in advance. Poor Lisa had known me an hour and had seen a side to me that I didn't even know existed. Hudson was looking at me in shock, he had never seen me angry before. That boy had brought me so much joy — I never got angry with him.

The manager of the Virgin lounge had been informed of the situation Lachlan and I were in, and had offered for us to all sit in the Virgin lounge until our flight was ready for boarding. We agreed and made our way to the lounge. We weren't about to leave Lisa behind, so she got in as well. As soon as I walked into the lounge, I saw all the alcohol in the fridge. I desperately wanted a drink, but I knew I would probably end up in prison if I went down that road, so I stuck with water instead. Hudson was having a great time, running around, eating and playing with another little kid. He was completely unaware of what was happening.

We sat in the Alice Springs airport for nine hours before we finally boarded the plane, which was the original plane we landed in Alice Springs on anyway. The flight felt like it went for ten hours but we arrived safely in Adelaide with two minutes to spare before the cut off time for incoming flights. Ethel met us outside the airport and took us back to her house. It was almost 11pm once we arrived at her house. Hudson was used to being in bed by 7pm, so he passed out as soon as I laid him in the porta cot. I stayed up for another two hours preparing the perfect slide show of photos for the funeral.

The next morning, I was up at 6am, I felt like shit, looked like shit and didn't want today to even be here. Simone texted me to say *'good luck'* – she was on holiday in Melbourne and couldn't make the funeral. Lachlan and I arrived at the funeral home early so we could set up the slide show, which wouldn't work. I was starting to get angry. All I wanted was the perfect slide show for my beautiful boy, but it just wasn't happening. People were arriving, which made me go and hide in the toilet. I didn't want to see anyone; I didn't want to show emotion in front of them. I had a cry in the toilet, pulled myself together then went to start speaking to the guests. Shelby had arrived, which was great to see. She always had severe anxiety in front of large crowds, so I wasn't expecting to see her. Shalanda and Rikki-Lee turned up with Dad and Kay – it was so good to see Shalanda and cuddle her. She knew exactly what I was going through, and it gave me a bit of comfort knowing she was there if I needed her. There were lots of new faces arriving, which was Lachlan's side of the family. I didn't want to meet anyone – every time I met someone new, it felt like they were up in my face. I didn't remember any of their names either. Ethel grabbed me as I walked past her.

'Jasmin, you haven't even met my father yet,' she said as she rolled her eyes.

I don't know if she meant to be rude, but she sure as hell came across that way. I smiled, said *'hello'* then quickly walked away.

I went and sat at the front of the room, where Bryson's teddy bear urn sat with his ashes in it. There was also a beautiful picture of him in a frame next to the urn. Rick announced that the service was starting. Everyone sat down, Dad sat next to me, with Mum alongside him, while Ethel sat next to Lachlan with Ron next to her. There wasn't a lot that Rick could say about Bryson. I mean, he didn't even get the chance to take his first breath, so there wasn't much he could say. I did write a poem for Bryson which Rick read out, which was followed by four songs that Lachlan and myself had picked.

'Somewhere Over the Rainbow' by Israel Kamakawiwo'ole was played first. I sat there listening to people sobbing but not one tear fell from my eyes, I thought there was something wrong with me, I just couldn't cry. The second song to play was 'Fix You' by Coldplay, the exact song I was hearing when I dreamt about being at my baby's funeral. The only difference was, there wasn't a coffin.

The third song to play was an interesting choice by Lachlan and I. Lachlan mentioned that his dad loved the song and when I heard it for the first time, I definitely wanted it played. It was called 'It's a Motherfucker' by The Eels. It is such a beautiful song with a lot of meaning about death and grief behind it. Once the song finished, Rick mentioned that he had never heard that song at a funeral but it was definitely very suitable for Bryson's death. He asked if anyone wanted to get up and say a few words. No one moved for a good 30 seconds. It was so awkward, but Dad decided to get up and say a few things. He mentioned that he was my dad and that he couldn't even imagine laying me to rest. He also went on to say that he loved Lachlan and Bryson, that he would miss Bryson. It made me smile, it was nice to hear someone else say they were going to miss my boy. The very last song to play was 'Tears in Heaven' by Eric Clapton. Rick asked everyone to stand, take a rose petal from the table and place it into the little box that Bryson's urn would sit in. By this stage I was feeling like the worst mother. I was, of course, devastated. People could see that, but I still couldn't cry. As Lachlan and I held hands and made our way to the back of the room where Hudson was playing, I told Lachlan that I didn't cry, and it turns out he didn't either.

We held onto our emotions that day. We thought that maybe we just wanted everyone else to grieve today and we would do it later on, together. After everyone had placed a rose petal into the box, we all wrote a note to Bryson. We attached them to balloons, made our way outside and let our balloons go at the same time. Lachlan had tied his and my balloons together, and we watched them float off on their own, while all the other balloons stayed in a pack.

'Do you think Bryson is guiding our balloons honey?' Lachlan asked, I just smiled and nodded.

We had a small get together at a local pub after the funeral. Not a lot of people turned up, which I was very much ok with. I just sat inside while everyone else stayed outside to eat and drink. I was so exhausted from the whole day; we left the pub early. Once we were back at Ethel's place, I put Hudson down for a nap, grabbed Bryson's urn and held it so tight, until I fell asleep.

Two days later it was Christmas Day. I woke up knowing I wasn't going to be in the best of moods, I didn't want anything to do with Christmas celebrations and neither did Lachlan. All of Hudson's Christmas presents were back in Darwin so he didn't have anything to open, and Bryson was dead, so we were just feeling so down. Lachlan and I were meant to make an appearance at his grandmother's house for lunch. I suggested that he go and I stay home, but he didn't want to go anywhere either. Ethel asked us what our plans were for the day and when Lachlan told her we were staying home, she yelled at him. She told us to stop being sad sacks. I didn't understand how or why she wasn't being more supportive and understanding, it wasn't until Lachlan told me that Ethel had never actually lost anyone close to her in her life. It was difficult being around someone who had never grieved. I had to try my best to put my grief on hold, just until we went back home, which was so hard, especially when I was still pumping milk and missing Bryson so much. Ethel sat with me while I was pumping my milk and gave me some really good advice.

'Jasmin, what you are doing is amazing, but look how miserable you are, you aren't enjoying this experience, maybe it's time you stopped.'

Ethel didn't understand my grief but she could clearly see it, so I took her advice and stopped donating my milk. I felt like I had let little Sophie down, just like I let Lachlan down when Bryson died.

Boxing Day was Lachlan's birthday. I took him out for dinner, and all we talked about was Bryson. Three days after Lachlan's birthday was Hudson's 2nd birthday. I wanted him to have a great day, he was also suffering, he was the one watching his mum and dad suffer and didn't have a clue as to why. We took him to a little animal farm for the day, it was such a hot summer's day but that didn't stop him from running around with the animals, milking cows and patting the baby rabbits. I smiled as I watched my now two-year-old having the time of his life, but in the back of my mind, I kept wishing that Bryson was here too.

New Year's Eve was just the same as any other day since Bryson had left us. I had put Hudson to bed at 7pm, got myself a can of coke and sat outside with Ethel, Ron and Lachlan. A conversation was brought up by Ethel about the possibility of me having OCD, because I was always putting Hudson to bed at the same time. I shook my head in disbelief, there was no way she was going to start on my parenting a few days after my son's funeral. I looked over at Ron and Lachlan, with my head slightly down and said, '*I don't have OCD*'.

I think I was hoping Ethel was just a little drunk and talking nonsense, but Ron and Lachlan both looked at me and agreed with Ethel. I wanted to cry. I was extremely hurt, mainly at Lachlan for agreeing. As far as I was aware, Lachlan and I co-parented really well. After our OCD chat, I wasn't feeling the best, so I went to bed and cried and cried. I always hated crying, but since Bryson had died, I found myself doing it a lot more and I absolutely hated it. I heard Lachlan and Ethel walking into the kitchen area which was near the room I was sleeping in. I had the door cracked open enough where I could hear everything that was being said. Ethel was explaining to Lachlan how selfish I was.

'She didn't even say goodnight,' she snapped. 'Jasmin needs to understand that she isn't the only one hurting, it's not all about her.'

I could hear Lachlan saying, 'Ok Mum, I'll talk to her'.

Why the fuck did I leave the door open that night? I wish I never heard any of that conversation, it was the conversation that tipped me over the edge. I felt the depression and anger hit me so hard that night. I laid in bed for hours stewing on everything in my life. My sexual abuse, Mum not helping me, Tom being an asshole, Bryson dying and now Ethel. I could literally feel the anger taking over my body.

I confronted Lachlan about the conversation I overheard. He apologised but I was too furious to forgive him.

'Why didn't you stick up for me?' I asked.

Lachlan shrugged his shoulders and said, 'Because sometimes it's better to just agree with Mum so she shuts up'.

I knew instantly that he was afraid of his mother. He didn't admit it but it was clear. Everything that had been said that night, I stored in my head, and locked it up. I knew eventually that I could talk to Ethel about what she said, but now wasn't the right time. We spent a month

The tipping point

in South Australia. I was so happy to be returning home where I could start to let out some of the grief I had been hiding away.

The second we landed back in Darwin, I felt so much relief. Hudson unwrapped all of his Christmas presents while I took down the Christmas tree. I set up a little memorial shelf for Bryson in the lounge room. It had a teddy bear, his urn and a little glass jar filled with all of the rose petals that everyone placed in Bryson's box at the funeral. I received a text just after we returned home from my old boss at the supermarket asking if I would like to return to work. At the time I thought it would be a great idea, it would keep my mind off of everything and I could move forward with my life quicker.

I gave myself three weeks of just being at home before I went back. I needed to do something with all of Bryson's things. I started to pack away his clothes, bassinet, the little hand and foot prints that the midwives had done for us while we were in hospital. As I started to put away everything into boxes, I came across Bryson's hospital bag. It hadn't been unpacked, and I was staring at it wondering if I should open it or not. It needed to be unpacked at some stage, so I opened it up and I instantly smelt Bryson. It was the smell of a newborn baby. I could see his little blanket in a plastic bag. I pulled it out, it had his blood on it, I rested my face on the blanket, and all I could smell was him. I called out to Lachlan to come and smell the blanket.

'What can you smell?' I asked as I put the blanket to his face.

'Bryson,' he whispered.

I burst into tears, *'Why the fuck did he die?'*

I cried out as I wiped my tears on the blanket. Lachlan grabbed me and cuddled me so tight.

'I don't know why, but it fucking sucks,' he said as he fought back his own tears. I was scared to have the blanket out too long just in case his smell went away, so I quickly put the blanket back into the plastic bag, zipped up the hospital bag and put it on my shelf in the walk-in wardrobe. There was no way I was going to unpack that bag; I wasn't ready at all.

Lachlan and I both started back at work around the same time. He worked in the morning and as soon as he finished, I would go to work, which meant Hudson always had one of us with him.

My first shift back was a hard one. I didn't even think about all of the regular customers who were going to ask me about my baby. Every single customer who asked me about Bryson got an honest answer. I was making grown men run out of the shop speechless. I didn't want them to feel bad, but I couldn't just lie to them and say the birth

The tipping point

was great and the baby is healthy. One of my favourite customers was a man named Steve. He would come in almost every day, he was always so happy and friendly.

'You're back at work already,' he said when he walked through the shop doors and saw me.

I just smiled and said, *'Yep, I missed the place'*.

Steve grabbed a drink from the fridge and made his way down to the front counter. He asked if I had a boy or a girl, I told him it was a beautiful baby boy. He then asked, *'So, all good then?'* I shook my head.

He began to say, *'No, don't you dare say it'*. I told him my son had died. Steve cried, I raced around the counter and cuddled him and we cried together. Steve was the only person to ask me about my son and not run away when I said that he died.

Steve left the shop still crying, and I was left feeling like someone finally cared.

Lachlan and I had begun to notice that our friends and family who said they were going to be there for us had gone back to their everyday lives, while we were left standing still in a land of grief and with no one to support us. That's why I was shocked when Steve cried, he was my customer. I barely knew him, but he cared.

As the weeks went by, I would either sit at home all day with Hudson or I would go into the city and browse through the shops. I would spark up a conversation with the salesperson, and mention Bryson to them. I wanted them to know that I loved my son and I missed him. The conversations never lasted long, probably because I would make the other person feel super uncomfortable. I wanted to bring Bryson up all the time, to anyone and everyone. Thankfully Lachlan enjoyed listening and talking about him too, so we would sit for hours and talk about my pregnancy and his birth. It made us both feel better, just for that little while.

Being at home most of the time was driving me insane. Simone was working a lot so I wasn't seeing her very often, and staring at four walls was making me angry. I went out the back one afternoon and saw that our grass needed to be mowed. *'That will keep me busy,'* I thought as I grabbed the lawn mower off the back veranda. As I tried to start it, it died. I looked into the fuel tank and there was no fuel. Seeing that there was no fuel in the lawn mower sent me into a rage. I stormed over to the patch of grass and began to rip it out with my bare hands, I was pulling as hard as I could, the sweat was pouring out of me. I started to get angrier as I struggled to pull the grass out. In the meantime, Lachlan had come home for lunch. I was standing inside, sculling a bottle of water, covered in dirt and grass. He asked what had happened and I just broke down.

The tipping point

'I want Bryson here,' I cried.

'He is here Jazz, he is with us,' Lachlan replied.

I stormed into the lounge room and screamed, *'No he is a pile of fucking ashes in our lounge room! He isn't in heaven or in our hearts, he is fucking dead.'*

I went over to the kitchen bench and began to grab whatever I could and throw it across the kitchen.

Lachlan let me go. He let me get out all of my anger. Once I stopped hurling shit across the room, I sat on the floor. Lachlan sat with me.

I looked at him and said, *'I don't think I can go on living without my son'.*

Chapter 11

A surprise wedding

The time had come to find out Bryson's autopsy results. Lachlan and I went to the hospital and met with a midwife who I hadn't dealt with when it came to my pregnancy with Bryson or my birth, which was disappointing. We wanted someone who we had dealt with before to give us the results, but I guess it didn't matter who told us how he died. Lachlan and I were still going to feel the same way.

The midwife began to explain that Bryson died from a 'cord accident'. His umbilical cord was wrapped around his neck twice.

'So, my son choked to death,' I snapped at the midwife as Lachlan held my hand, stroking my fingers, trying to keep me calm.

Then I remembered Carol, the midwife who talked me out of having a C-section at 38 weeks.

I looked at Lachlan and said, *'This is my fault, I listened to that bitch midwife and now our son is dead'*.

I left the hospital that day with one thing on my mind; I wanted to see Carol. I wanted to ask her why she told me what to do with my own body, why her opinion mattered so much. Lachlan and I arranged a meeting with the patient advocate of the hospital, the lady in charge of the maternity ward, and the head midwife of the maternity ward. I had requested that Carol be at the meeting but I was very quickly shut down. I was told she was busy and couldn't attend.

Lachlan and I went over our concerns with the way Carol treated me the day I had my appointment with her, and why was my appointment being interrupted by another midwife, telling Carol to hurry up. We also spoke about the nurse throwing a bag of drugs at me before we left the hospital. Every concern we had, we were given excuses. Carol had told the patient advocate that she never said anything to me that would make me feel like I was being forced into a VBAC. The nurse had been spoken to about throwing drugs at me but she was new so she wasn't aware she was doing anything wrong. I sat in the chair listening to the excuses coming from the mouths of the "professionals" and I felt sick to my stomach. I felt

A surprise wedding

like these people were sad for Lachlan and I, but their reputations were more important and they would never admit any fault.

Lachlan and I had been having such a rough time with everything, we had forgotten about our wedding. It was my 30th birthday in April and I had organised a big party before Bryson died. People from other states were coming up for it, so I couldn't cancel. I didn't want to let anyone down. Lachlan suggested something else that we should do for my 30th.

'Why don't we have a surprise wedding?' he said.

We had planned to wait until Bryson was around six months old before we got married, but obviously that all turned to shit, so we figured why wait? I called Simone to tell her. She was my one and only bridesmaid, and I wanted her to be there when I was picking a dress.

Lachlan informed his best man, who was his childhood friend, Ben. We told most immediate family and that was it, no one else knew. We organised a fake engagement lunch the day before my 30th birthday party. We figured we would get married and then have a joint reception at my party.

Simone and I went to the local bridal store to try on some dresses. I didn't want to spend a mint on a dress, I just wanted something simple and short enough so I didn't trip over the it. As I was trying on dresses, nothing stood out to me, or to Simone, plus I hadn't worked out since I had Bryson so I had my baby weight clinging to me as well. The lovely lady who was helping me with the dresses brought over this long gown. It looked horrible, but she insisted I try it on. Simone was even giving me the eye, as if to say, *'Nope, it's ugly'*. I tried it on anyway, and as I came out of the fitting room and stood in front of the mirror, I fell in love with it. So did Simone. It fit so nicely on my hips, and once Simone had said it looked beautiful, I knew I was getting the dress.

The planning wasn't stressful. We had the venue booked, and we only invited a very small amount of people to the surprise wedding so we didn't have to worry about anything. Although I had some exciting times ahead, I was also feeling the grief hitting me so hard. Every time I would drive to work, I would picture myself just driving myself into a tree. These thoughts scared the absolute shit out of me, I had never had this in my life. I texted Simone about the thoughts. She didn't really say much about them – I think I may have scared the shit out of her too. I went to the doctor, but they just wanted me to go on anti-depressants, which I was dead against. I kept saying, *'I got through my childhood and Tom's mental abuse without drugs, so I can get through this too'*. I had always pulled myself out of shitty situations and in my eyes, I could get through the death of my son just fine.

A surprise wedding

It was two days before the wedding, and my family and friends had started arriving from all over Australia. Lachlan's best man and family arrived as well, including his grandmother, which made Lachlan so happy. My dad couldn't make it. He had no idea I was getting married, but I thought he was definitely coming for my 30th birthday so I kept the wedding a surprise from him, which totally blew up in my face. I had no one to walk me down the aisle. I was going to ask Mum's partner, Mike, but Ethel suggested that Ron walk me down the aisle. I wasn't really that keen on the idea. I hadn't known him long but I figured he had been in Lachlan's life long enough, so it may make Lachlan proud.

I was a nervous wreck this time around. Simone and I were walking into the hotel where the makeup artist was meeting us, and when we saw some of my family were eating breakfast, we laughed as we ran like hell, just in case they saw us. Everyone had been told that Lachlan I had to work for a few hours that day, but we would meet them at the engagement party. The crazy thing is, everyone believed us. Lachlan, Ben and Hudson all got ready down the hall in another hotel room. We had a videographer and a photographer capturing every moment. I had a photo of Bryson sitting in the room with me as I got ready. I wanted it to feel like he was right there with me. Hudson came to visit me just as I had my makeup and hair done. I bent down to give him a cuddle and he said *'Mummy'* as he stroked my face – I like to think that was his way of saying I looked beautiful.

Eventually, it was time for the boys to head to the venue and wait for guests to arrive. A couple of friends had caught on to what was really happening, a gut feeling, apparently. One friend texted and said, *'you sneaky bitch'*, with a winky emoji. Simone and I were having such a great time having our photos taken and chatting away to the photographer that we actually lost track of time. I looked at the clock and realised I was 20 minutes late for my own wedding. We ran downstairs where my car had been waiting, jumped in and off we went.

The closer we got to the venue, the more nervous I felt. I was shaking. When we arrived, Simone and I got out of the car, and headed for the front door of the venue. Ron stood there waiting for me. He linked arms with me and said, *'Are you ready?'*

'I sure am,' I replied.

The music started, Ruth and Hudson walked through then Simone and Ben but I was still outside, so no one could see me. Lachlan had always wanted the song 'Dela' by Johnny Clegg from George of the Jungle played at his wedding, and after a week of protesting, I decided it was actually a great song to walk down the aisle to. As soon as the chorus started, I began to walk through the doors.

Ron laughed and said, *'Slow down, it's not a marathon'*.

A surprise wedding

I was walking so fast, because I was so damn nervous! I looked over at Lachlan, he was standing there with the biggest smile on his face. I looked at Hudson, who was trying to escape from my mum's arms so he could come and cuddle me and I thought, *'Now this time feels right'*. Seven years ago I had said I would marry Lachlan, and here I was, about to be his wife.

As soon as I had reached Lachlan, I asked him to hold my hands the entire time. My legs were shaking so bad, I thought I would fall down if he let go of me. The ceremony was short but lovely. Lachlan read out his vows, and I melted – he had definitely taken his time to make sure they were perfect. When it was my turn to say mine, I grabbed the microphone and said, *'Well mine are just going to sound crap now'*, and everyone laughed.

As I said my vows, I got really emotional, I burst into tears halfway through. I surprised myself with how much emotion I had running through me. The marriage celebrant mentioned Bryson and Lachlan's dad watching our special day from above. I looked at Lachlan and I could see that comment really hit his heart. He was only 26 and had lost two really important people in his life. After we both said *'I do'* we celebrated with our family and friends. Simone and Ben both made a speech, and Simone began to cry at the end of hers. It was really sweet, you could tell how happy she was for us both. As everyone was mingling, I noticed that Ethel had been avoiding me, she didn't congratulate to me either. I was really getting the hint now that she didn't like me. I always thought maybe it was because I never came from money or I was a little bit bogan, but whatever it was, she made it clear the day I married her son.

After stopping at my favourite pub in Darwin after the wedding, we all went out for a quiet dinner, then Lachlan and I went back to a hotel that Ron had shouted us as a wedding gift. We stripped out of our wedding gear and did something we liked to do most nights – talk about Bryson. We wondered what he would have looked like in his suit standing next to Hudson. As much as it was a sad topic, it felt healthy for us to always talk about Bryson with each other.

The next day was my 30th party/wedding reception. More people were coming to this party. I was excited to see everyone, and I knew that night would keep my mind off of Bryson and I might be able to just relax. Ethel, Ron and Lachlan's grandma flew home the morning of my party, but Ruth stayed for the party. She wanted to help us celebrate. The night started off great, lots of people turned up, but a lot of people left early to go to the pub. I was left with the closest people to me which actually turned out well. We finished the night off with loads of dancing and laughing. I was home by midnight and eating left over birthday cake, what more could a girl want? All of the celebrations were over, which meant everyone was going home and back to their lives. I knew what that meant for me – back to being alone with my thoughts. I was ok for a couple of days, I even went for small runs to clear my head if I was starting to feel really depressed, but none of it lasted long. I would always end up feeling like shit and distancing myself from people.

Simone and I were still seeing each other but not very often. She hadn't mentioned any wedding plans to me since Bryson died. At first, I didn't notice but as the months went on I started to wonder if maybe I wasn't going to be her bridesmaid after all. I ended up texting Simone one afternoon at work asking if I was still one of her bridesmaids, and she texted back letting me know I was no longer a part of her bridal party. She couldn't afford for me to be in the wedding. I was absolutely devasted, I sat in the office crying my heart out. I didn't want to push her on the subject and I wasn't going to beg her to change her mind, she had obviously had this on her mind for a while but didn't want to tell me, so I just let it go.

After that, I didn't see Simone at all. I really felt like my grief had pushed her away and I felt incredibly guilty. I needed to get away from Darwin for a while, I needed to go on a nice road trip and just forget about everything. Simone had called Lachlan after our road trip was locked in. I hadn't answered her texts for two days, so she called Lachlan to see if I was ok. Lachlan mentioned the road trip to her, to which Simone replied with, *'Jasmin's always been one to run away from her problems. She's a flight risk.'*

I didn't know any of that was said until a week later when we had just started our long trip to Adelaide. When Lachlan mentioned it, I went silent. When I'm silent, I'm usually at my angriest. How could my best friend say that I run away from my problems? I couldn't run away from Bryson dying, I couldn't run away from the grief, I was faced with it every day, no matter what side of the planet I was on. Simone just didn't get it because she had never grieved like I was.

That night I went on social media and dropped some very subtle hints that I knew what Simone had said, and she blocked me instantly. I hated her for not even explaining herself or apologising. I was angry at myself as well, for not being the same person I used to be. I kept saying, *'If Bryson lived, this shit wouldn't be happening. I wish I could have saved him.'* That was all I would say, over and over. Eight years of having a sister and a best friend all rolled into one went down the toilet.

I didn't want Simone cutting me off to upset our road trip, so I decided to just move on, like I did with everything else in my life, and enjoy some time in Adelaide with Lachlan. Mike's mum was visiting Darwin and had offered to take care of Hudson so Lachlan and I could spend some quality time together. As much as I didn't want to leave Hudson, I knew Lachlan and I needed it.

A surprise wedding

All the way to Adelaide I was craving coffee, the cold weather made me want to drink it, which was causing me to bloat. I looked five months pregnant all the time. I would rub my belly and tell Lachlan it was my coffee baby. We spent three days in Adelaide, we saw Ruth, Ethel and Ron. Ethel was nice to me, we chatted about Bryson and about Lachlan and I being posted to Perth with Defence. We were 100% ready to get the hell out of Darwin, which Ethel understood completely. I started to think that I was wrong about Ethel, she didn't speak to me at my wedding but maybe we were both caught up chatting to other people. Ron was my go-to guy for a coffee whenever I wanted one – he had the best coffee machine. Ruth took us out for lunch the day before we left, and we had Chinese. I was craving wonton soup, which made me laugh because that was one of my main cravings I had when I was pregnant with Hudson.

After a very short trip to Adelaide, it was time to head home to Hudson. The drive felt longer heading home than what it was leaving it, mainly because my lower back was in so much pain all the way home. I drove Lachlan crazy with my whinging about the pain, not to mention my requests for coffee every few hours.

As soon as we got home, we picked up Hudson. It almost looked like he had grown taller in the short amount of time we were gone. We knew we needed food for the house, so we went grocery shopping before heading home.

Hudson walked around the supermarket, helping us put the groceries in the trolley. We got to the biscuit aisle, and I grabbed a packet of chicken crimpy shapes and chucked them in the trolley. Lachlan grabbed my arm with his eyes wide open – I was looking at him with a rather confused look on my face. He asked why I was buying the chicken crimpy biscuits. I thought he was losing his mind. I was buying them because I had a craving for them earlier that day, which made Lachlan think I was pregnant.

'You hate chicken crimpy; you only ate them when you were pregnant with Bryson,' Lachlan said as I grabbed an extra packet of chicken crimpy. I didn't feel pregnant. I knew my body and I wasn't pregnant but I grabbed a pregnancy test anyway. I hid it from Lachlan, because I didn't want to take it and have to tell him it was negative. I could see it in his eyes that he wanted me to be pregnant, and I couldn't bear to let him down again. I loaded the shopping onto the checkout, hiding the test under a packet of pads, which probably looked a little weird to the checkout chick. I distracted Lachlan with my normal chit chat as the test was scanned and bagged, we paid for our shopping then made our way home.

Lachlan went outside to take the washing off the line while I unpacked everything. I found the test and took it straight away. I hid it behind the little bin in the toilet, just in case Lachlan came back inside. The test was flashing and flashing and fucking flashing, it took forever. As I went to pick it up, thinking it was a dud, the result popped up. It said 'yes' with a plus sign. I was left gobsmacked; I was sure I wasn't pregnant. I started to shake and cry, I closed my eyes and whispered, *'Thank you Bryson'.*

As I opened up the back door, Lachlan turned to look at me with a pile of washing in his hands and I said, *'Well, you're going to be a Dad again'*. Lachlan dropped the pile of washing, ran over to me, looked at the test and said, *'I bloody knew it'*. We cuddled and cried together; we were happy but so scared at the same time.

I wasted no time telling everyone this time, we did everything right last time and our baby still died, so what was the point of waiting for that safe zone. In our eyes, there never is a safe zone.

It must have been three days after I announced my pregnancy that I started to bleed. I got up one morning to pee, and I heard something dripping into the toilet as soon as I sat down. I looked in the toilet to find blood everywhere. I shouted out to Lachlan, who was still asleep. He got up and ran into the toilet. I had to tell my husband that I was losing another one of his babies.

We went straight to the emergency room, where we were taken in for an ultrasound. The lady who was about to perform my ultrasound mentioned that she didn't usually perform them because she was a doctor, and she was the only one available at the time. I couldn't bear to even look at the screen once the ultrasound began, I knew I was going to be told I had miscarried. Lachlan tapped me on the arm and told me to look at the screen. I saw a little baby on the screen and what looked like a second sack right next to it. I mentioned the second sack, but the doctor was adamant that it was a cyst and that's why I was bleeding so much. Lachlan and I couldn't believe that our baby was alive.

Once everything was checked over and baby was given the ok, we were asked to wait in the waiting room for our results. The doctor had to send them off to be looked over properly before we could go. The same doctor handed us our paperwork. It was all sealed up, nothing was explained, so I assumed it was a cyst. We said thank you and were sent on our merry way. I didn't even think to look at the paperwork. We knew our baby was safe and that's all that mattered.

Little did I know that there was very important information in that envelope that I wouldn't read until almost two years later.

The time had come to move to Perth. I was so angry at the patient advocate at the hospital, I had called her recently to try and organise another meeting with her and Carol. I had explained that I just wanted to explain my pain and concerns, but I was told I would get a call back the following day. That day didn't come. My morning sickness was kicking my ass, I wasn't spewing this time but I felt so sick and extremely exhausted – I just slept in between packing. Leaving Darwin was sad but now that I was pregnant, I knew we were doing the right thing, and there was not a chance in hell that I would ever have another baby in the hospital there – I wasn't going to risk it. I didn't say goodbye to anyone when we left, I was so done with Darwin and the grief that was there. I just wanted to get to Perth and start fresh and to get the best possible treatment for the baby as I possibly could.

Chapter 12

Irreplaceable

Pulling up to our new house in Perth felt strange. We were the only people who lived on the street – all the other houses were still being built or had no occupants yet. I was looking forward to living in a nice street with other families, and hopefully making some friends but it looked like that may not happen anytime soon. Lachlan had to go straight back to work once we moved in to our place. I slowly unpacked a box or two each day, but for some reason I just didn't want to set the entire house up. I left boxes of stuff in our spare room, and didn't hang anything on the walls or make the house very homely. I made Hudson's little bed up in mine and Lachlan's room. I didn't want him to sleep away from me, I was so paranoid that he would die in his sleep or someone would break in and kidnap him. I put Bryson's hospital bag safely in my room. Everything inside was still untouched but I couldn't bring myself to open the bag again, not yet.

Hudson became bored quite quickly at home, he would yell out to me, *'Mum, come play with me'*, but I was too busy laying on the couch crying. It was a mixture of things. Bryson, Simone, being pregnant again. Everything was just eating away at me. I thought I would put Hudson into day care, that way I could have some time to just focus on me and try to control my grief. Like it was going to be that easy. Hudson would go to day care two days a week, and those two days I spent crying all day, eating anything that I could get my hands on, and stewing on everything that had happened in my whole life. I would think all day long, it would become so depressing. I would go on social media and write about Bryson, and feel guilty doing it because I knew people would be sick of seeing his name or me talking about him. I would receive messages from people saying things like,

'Why are you so sad? You can have another 20 babies if you wanted,' 'Stop feeling sorry for yourself,' 'You are so strong, you'll be fine'. All of these comments were made by people who hadn't suffered the loss of a baby, but I found myself trying to take their advice.

'Ok, you have got to be strong, prove to these people that you are strong and you will get through all of this just fine.'

Those are the the kinds of things I would think, instead of just allowing myself to grieve properly; I tried so hard to keep blocking it out. Every single ultrasound appointment I had, Lachlan would come along, and I would do the same thing at every appointment. I would get onto the bed, turn my head away from the ultrasound screen, close my eyes so tight and pray the baby wasn't dead. I would hold Lachlan's hand and sweat a cold sweat as I waited for the sonographer to find a heartbeat. Every time I would hear that my little baby was ok, my whole body would relax. I would turn my head back to the ultrasound and smile as I watched he or she moving and kicking. As happy as I was that the baby was ok, I just couldn't bring myself to connect. I didn't spend my time buying cute little outfits online like I did with Bryson, or get excited about a new pram and installing a car seat. None of that mattered to me anymore. I had myself convinced that I would have another stillbirth. It was only a matter of time before this baby would die too.

A couple of months had gone by since we moved to Perth and I absolutely hated the place; I didn't want to be there at all. I couldn't bear to be alone with my thoughts. I could feel the suicidal thoughts coming on really strong. I would pick up a knife to cut a sandwich, look at the knife and imagine just stabbing myself straight in the heart. It would end all of this shit in my head, the shit no one wants to carry around every single day. I opened up to Lachlan about my thoughts and he took me straight to hospital. I was sent over to the mental health facility to talk to a psychologist. I begged and begged for a pill to make me better, for someone to help me feel better so I could be normal again. The psychologist told me how common it was for grieving parents to ask exactly what I did and that there was no magical pill to stop the grief, I just had to go through the motions. I didn't want to, I just wanted to stop this fucking nightmare, NOW! I was told about antidepressants, but again, I refused to know about them.

'They won't work, I need something else,' I would cry – something that would make me forget. I would always say I wish I had amnesia after Bryson died, I just couldn't bear to think about him anymore, it hurt too much. I was asked how my sleep was going. I hadn't slept properly since Bryson died, I would be up at 2am thinking about him until daylight or I just wouldn't sleep at all. I was offered to stay the night but I just wanted to go home, I wanted to be in my own bed.

Lachlan stayed home with me for a couple of days which helped me so much. Having him with me made me feel that slightest bit better. I had always been so independent so relying on someone to make me feel better was such a weird feeling for me. It made me feel like a failure in a way too. Once Lachlan went back to work and Hudson was at day care, I sat in the kitchen, stuffing myself with KFC, thinking about the patient advocate back in Darwin who never called me back when she said she would. It had been months since I heard from her, so I decided to put in a formal complaint regarding the fact she ignored my request for another meeting.

It must have been about 20 minutes after the complaint was sent in, when I received a call from a mobile number. On the other end was a midwife from Darwin. I had never met this midwife but she had told me that the patient advocate tried calling me a lot a few weeks ago, and I never called her back. I couldn't help myself, I had to tell this midwife exactly what I thought which was *'What a load of fucking shit'*. I was also told that Carol was too busy to talk to me but she passed on her condolences. The blood boiling inside of me was like a volcano about to erupt. Carol couldn't even step up and listen to what I had to say. She had no backbone, no empathy, but I can guarantee she had a guilty fucking conscience. Carol was able to hide behind her bosses and the patient advocate. Carol was protected whilst Lachlan and I were left to suffer.

Lachlan had come home from work later that day to me in a rage. I was so angry about Carol and her being too fucking gutless to even face me, *'Guilty fucking conscience, that cunt has a guilty fucking conscience'*. I wanted Bryson's death to haunt her, just like it did to me. Lachlan grabbed me and cuddled me so tight.

'All of this sucks Jasmin, but you need to stop stressing out. It's just not healthy for you or the baby,' he said.

Sometimes I would forget I was pregnant; I had the belly but I chose to ignore it most of the time. One thing we couldn't ignore was finding out the baby's gender. We had an appointment the very next day to see if we were having a boy or a girl. I had ordered two white baseballs, one was filled with pink chalk, the other filled with blue. My friend, Kay, who I went to school with, was living in Perth, and had offered to film the reveal. First Lachlan and I went in for my ultrasound. I did my same routine of looking away from the screen and waited for the sonographer to tell me that the baby was either dead or alive. Thankfully everything was ok, I smiled at Lachlan as he kissed my hand with the look of relief in his eyes. The sonographer wrote the gender on a note pad, sealed it in an envelope and off we went to meet Kay for the big reveal. Kay had read the note, got the right ball out of the box, handed it to me, and Lachlan was ready with his baseball bat. Kay got my phone ready to record, and gave me the signal to throw the ball. I looked at Lachlan and said, *'You ready?'* he nodded and I threw the ball.

Lachlan smashed the ball and out came a huge cloud of blue chalk dust. I ran over to Lachlan and threw myself into his arms. We were absolutely stoked to be having another boy! I called my dad as soon as I got home to tell him I was having another boy; Dad was excited for

Lachlan and I but he said something that made me shake my head in disbelief.

'Oh good, now you can replace the one you lost Jazz.'

'No Dad, it doesn't work like that, Bryson is irreplaceable,' I replied.

Dad apologised; he didn't mean it to come out that way but it hurt me a lot. No one on the planet could replace my baby, Bryson. Telling Hudson about having a little brother didn't go the way I had planned either. After I told him, he looked me dead in the eye and said, *'Can I have a biscuit?'*

I looked at Lachlan as he was smiling away at my belly and said, *'Ah well, at least you're excited'*.

After the enjoyment of having another boy had worn off, I went straight back to the messy grieving person I did not want to be. I needed to leave, I needed to go home to Darwin. I just wanted to go back to my old life in Darwin and forget I even went to Perth. I felt like I had absolutely no one around me. I told Lachlan that I had to leave Perth, I couldn't be there anymore. I didn't want to have another baby in Darwin, but I needed to get the fuck out of the hellhole I was in. Having no support when Lachlan was working was too painful to bear anymore. Lachlan knew I was serious; he knew I was going to leave but he wasn't going to let me go alone. He went to work the very next day and asked to be posted to a different state. He didn't tell me until it was approved. We had the choice of Darwin or Adelaide. As much as I missed life in Darwin, Lachlan and I just couldn't allow another one of our children to be born there. I thanked Lachlan for organising the posting. It was such a relief to be going to Adelaide – Shelby was there and Lachlan's family too.

We spent another month in Perth, and I spent almost that entire month crying. Bryson's 1st birthday was coming up, and I was absolutely dreading it. Other grieving mums had warned me that the 1st birthday is the hardest. On Bryson's actual birthday, I was fine. I had cried so much that I had nothing left to give. I spent the day making cupcakes and just embracing time with Lachlan and Hudson. Bryson never once left my mind that day. I wondered what sort of birthday cake he would have had, if he would still have his beautiful black curly hair, what it would feel like to cuddle him and hear his voice. Those were things I could only ever imagine. They were never going to be a reality, my reality was that my son was gone, and never coming back. It was painful to think about it that way, but it was the cold hard truth.

Lachlan and I did so well to keep ourselves together on Bryson's birthday, but now it was time to pack up and get ready to move. Thankfully I never unpacked the house properly, it made the packing so much smoother. Dad stopped by on our final day in Perth to say goodbye. I wasn't expecting him so it was lovely to see him. As Dad got in his car he said, *'Make sure you have that baby on my birthday'*. I laughed as he drove away, with his hand out the window waving.

'Bye Dad, and goodbye Perth,' I yelled out with excitement. I hoped for a much better future in Adelaide, for my family's sake.

Chapter 13

Rainbows and postnatal

The drive to Adelaide was a long one. I had brought Bryson's little urn that was full of his ashes. I never trusted the removalists with them, so whenever we moved, Bryson came with us. As Bryson's urn sat at my feet, I wondered if other people would find it weird that we were travelling with our son's ashes. I found it so normal. I'm sure other grieving parents found it normal too, but right in the back of my mind I wondered if someone who had never suffered such a loss would think I was crazy. Maybe I was crazy?

We stopped in a little town called Coffin Bay which was right near my home town of Port Lincoln. Coffin Bay is such a beautiful spot. We walked down the beach and let Hudson play in the sand. I looked out into the crystal blue water and thought that maybe it was time to spread Bryson's ashes here. Lachlan's father had some of his ashes spread in Coffin Bay, so I thought it might be nice to leave Bryson with his grandpa. I spoke to Lachlan about it which made him go into a panic.

'I'm not ready to say goodbye yet,' he said as he wiped tears from his eyes. *'I just can't Jasmin.'*

There was no way I could tip all of Bryson's ashes into the ocean after seeing Lachlan so devastated. He was happy to spread some if we both spread a little bit each, so that's what we did. As Hudson ran through the water, laughing and looking for shells, Lachlan and I both took turns in saying goodbye to a tiny piece of our boy. It was peaceful. I wanted him to be free and happy.

In between moving, we had Christmas then Lachlan and Hudson's birthday. I managed to keep myself together for all three of those events. I just didn't want to ruin a special day with my own demons anymore.

Getting to Adelaide and settling into our new home was quite nice. We had a little house with a big yard, a cubby house for Hudson and a nice frangipani tree out the front. I felt like maybe this could be my chance to get my shit together and start feeling normal again, but with only a month to go until the baby was due, I was riddled with anxiety. I started to stress about baby's movements. One day he wasn't moving enough and the next he was moving too much. I was racing up to the hospital telling the midwives that I was sure my baby had died. I spent hours sitting in birthing suites with the baby's heart beat being monitored. I felt like a burden all the time but I wasn't risking anything this time. I couldn't cope if this baby died too.

Which is why Lachlan and I decided not to allow anyone near the baby for the first few weeks of his life if they weren't vaccinated against whooping cough. Ethel and Ron were against vaccinations and weren't happy about our decision. When I was pregnant with Bryson, I remember Lachlan telling me that he wasn't sure about Ethel being near the baby once he was born because she wasn't vaccinated properly. At that stage, I wasn't bothered about people not being vaccinated, just as long as they weren't sick when they visited. Since Bryson's death my whole mind set had changed, I was on board with Lachlan this time. We just couldn't risk losing another baby. Ethel and Ron wanted Lachlan and I to see their point of view on not vaccinating and we wanted them to see our view on why we were going to vaccinate. None of us could agree on the others' opinion, so Lachlan and I just had to stand our ground and ask that Ethel and Ron stay away for eight weeks once the baby was born.

Ruth was great about the whole thing, she was vaccinated and couldn't wait to meet her nephew. My brother, Justin, had decided not to be vaccinated and understood why we needed him to wait a while before meeting his nephew. Shelby was another person who wasn't sure about being vaccinated. She kept saying, *'But I really want to meet my nephew and give him cuddles'*, and that's why she ended up getting the vaccination done. I wasn't expecting her to do it, so I was ecstatic when she went and got it done.

My first antenatal appointment at the women's and children's hospital was great, I was blown away with how professional everyone was. I had long appointments, the midwife would check myself and the baby over as thoroughly as she could to make sure we were both ok. I felt safe and was hopeful that maybe I would give birth to a living baby this time.

I was also given a date for my C-section, the 16th of February, which was a day before Dad's birthday. I laughed and said to Lachlan, *'That's close enough, surely that will keep him happy'*.

A week later I had another midwife appointment, after the baby's heartbeat was checked and everything was ok. The midwife asked if I knew about my C-section date changing. I was rather confused; I hadn't been told it had changed. The midwife went on to tell me that I was now having the baby on the 17th February, which was Dad's birthday. I was really excited after hearing that, but there was that thought in the back of my mind that, *'What if*

Rainbows and postnatal

the baby dies on Dad's birthday?' It would destroy him. I hated thinking like that, everything slightly positive turned into full blown anxiety and darkness.

My brain was wired that way now. I would sometimes sit for hours, thinking about dangerous situations that could happen with Hudson and then work out ways to save him. I thought of house fires, drownings, snake bites, anything you could think of, I had a well-thought out plan to save him from dying. Most of the things I would think about were bound to never happen but I had to be prepared.

The day had arrived to have my baby. I was 38 weeks pregnant and I was absolutely petrified. I had planned to unpack Bryson's hospital bag and use that, but I just couldn't bring myself to do it. I knew deep down that if I unpacked that bag, a huge piece of Bryson would leave me and I wasn't ready for that yet. We got a different bag with its own special meaning for this little baby instead.

Lachlan and I went to the hospital at 6am, whilst Hudson stayed home with my mum who had flown from Darwin to meet her newest grandson. I was the first person booked to have surgery. The lady at the desk signed me in, put a wrist band on me and asked if there was anything that she could do for me. I replied nervously with, *'Can you have the baby for me?'* She giggled and was very quick to let me know that she wasn't going to have my baby for me.

The Beauty in Bereavement

As Lachlan and I waited in pre-op, I looked at Lachlan in his scrubs with the biggest smile on his face. He was just so damn happy, it made me feel at ease seeing him that way. A nurse came through the curtains of our pre-op room and said, *'Are you ready sweetheart?'* I just nodded as she helped me off the bed and put her arm around me. This beautiful nurse had her arm around me the entire way to theatre, with Lachlan walking right beside us. When we arrived into theatre, I realised I had an all-female team. *'Girl power,'* I joked as I had the spinal block put into my back. I laid down on the bed, and waited for everything to go numb.

Lachlan pulled up a chair right next to me, held my hand and whispered, *'This time is going to be different and so special'*. I smiled at him, I couldn't talk. I was trying to focus on being calm. The time had come to cut me open. A nurse stood right next to me stroking my forehead.

'If you need anything, let me know,' she said.

I had my eyes shut for most of the surgery. I was thinking about Bryson's birth and how much I wished I was giving birth to him all over again, but with a happier ending. I suddenly opened my eyes when I felt that familiar tugging. The one where you feel like your organs are being pulled out. I knew the baby was almost here. The nurses dropped the safety curtain a little so I could see when the baby was born and I could see that he was ok.

I didn't need to see him to know he was fine, because at 9:04am he was born screaming the walls down. When the nurses showed me my beautiful, healthy baby boy, I went into shock. I was expecting a baby that looked like Bryson, but my son looked nothing like his brother at all. I started to shake uncontrollably. I couldn't talk, my teeth were chattering and I was freezing cold. The nurses got me warm blankets and put some medicine in my drip to stop the shaking. Lachlan was proud as punch holding his new born son, who we named Lincoln.

Once my shaking had stopped, I got to experience some skin on skin with Lincoln. It felt amazing to hold my son knowing I was going to take him home. After I was all stitched up and was being taken back to recovery, I thanked the team for giving me a healthy, living child. What was even better was having my son's face uncovered for everyone to see as I was wheeled into recovery. Lachlan started to call his family and tell them the news and I had the pleasure of calling Dad to wish him a happy birthday.

Dad asked what my plans were for the day and I responded with, *'Oh you know, I just had a baby'.*

Dad yelled down the phone, *'What? On my birthday? Finally, you listened to your old man, thank you Jasmin! This has made my whole day.'*

It felt great knowing Lincoln's birthday buddy was his poppy. Poor Lachlan wasn't getting the same sort of excitement from Ethel when he called her.

Ethel expressed how glad she was that Lincoln was born healthy but she was still not happy that we wouldn't allow her to see Lincoln yet. It made Lachlan and I sad that she just didn't get why we were so protective, but there was no way I was going to sit and think about that all day. We had a beautiful new son that we could hold and not have to leave without him. We were over the moon.

Breastfeeding was a bit of an issue from the get go. Lincoln latched properly but he would slip off my nipple. I had midwives trying to show me all different methods on how to breastfeed properly, which only became super overwhelming for me.

'I have breastfed before, why can't I do it this time?' I cried.

Lachlan took Lincoln, swaddled him up so perfectly and put him down for a sleep in his little crib.

I had visitors come and go all day. One very special visitor was Lincoln's big brother, Hudson. When Hudson walked in, Lincoln had started to get grizzly. Hudson looked at him and his lip started to drop.

'Is he ok Mummy?' Hudson asked. I had to explain that Lincoln was fine, he was just a bit tired.

Hudson was quite funny that day, he kept saying, *'Alright Mum, let's bring Lincoln home, are you ready to leave?'* I couldn't even feel my legs, so I wasn't going anywhere.

Once all the visitors stopped for the day, I felt absolutely knackered. I just wanted to go to sleep. I put Lincoln back on my breast to see if he could stay latched on. He latched for maybe three minutes, then slipped off. The midwives said he was latching fine which meant he was feeding fine but something told me he wasn't getting much from me, especially when he cried the entire two days we were in hospital. I just knew something wasn't right and as soon as we were discharged from hospital, Lachlan went and bought some formula. Lincoln drank the entire bottle, which made me think that I was starving my son in hospital. The guilt was so intense, I was convinced I had almost killed him.

As if I wasn't in a low enough mood, Ethel and Ron had called Lachlan to have another chat about vaccinations. Lachlan would just stand back and pretend to listen, just to keep them happy but I was getting angrier by the second.

'Give me that fucking phone,' I yelled.

Lachlan wouldn't hand me the phone. I was telling him to just hang up, and ignore the idiots.

'We have just brought our son home and they have managed to ruin that for us,' I yelled as Lachlan desperately tried to end the conversation with them.

Lachlan hung up, picked Lincoln up and just cried.

'Why don't they understand how precious this boy is to us?' he said as he kissed Lincoln's little hand.

I didn't have the answers, I didn't understand either. I was absolutely furious with Ethel and Ron, they turned a really magical moment for us into the Ethel and Ron show. Thankfully we had a friendly face at our door. Ruth had popped over to visit Lincoln, and she fell in love with him straight away. It was really cute seeing her hold Lincoln, being ever so gentle with him. Ruth had just fallen pregnant with twins, and Lachlan was proud as punch to know that Hudson and Lincoln would have cousins to play with. It was something to look forward to.

As the days went by, I found myself distancing myself from Lincoln. He would cry all day and all night, he just wanted to be held all the time and I didn't know why. Lachlan had to step up and take charge because I was locking myself away in my bedroom, thinking that any day now, Lincoln would die. Lachlan was doing all of the night feeds as I lay in bed crying. I couldn't bring myself to even feed my own son. Sometimes I would look at Lincoln and think, *'That's not my son'*.

Rainbows and postnatal

Lincoln's constant crying caused Lachlan and I some concern. A friend of mine suggested seeing a lactation consultant to check for tongue tie. I didn't even know what that was but I was willing to give anything a go to help settle Lincoln. A lactation consultant, Nicky, visited Lincoln. As soon as she opened his mouth, she could clearly see tongue, lip and cheek tie. Nicky said he was as stiff as an ironing board, which meant he was extremely stressed. We had to have the ties released straight away, so we found a dentist who lasered them off. It was the most horrific thing for a baby, but the results were amazing, Lincoln was like a brand-new baby by the time his ties had healed. He finally smiled at three months old, and took 15 minutes to drink a bottle instead of two hours.

He was starting to sleep better but there was still that one thing that wasn't right – me. I just couldn't bond with my son. He constantly wanted to be held and I just didn't want to get too close with him, anything could happen to him and I thought if I didn't bond with him than it wouldn't hurt so much if he died. Lachlan suggested I go to the doctor to have a chat; I knew exactly what the doctor would offer and I didn't want to go but I also knew I wasn't coping at all. I bit the bullet and booked the appointment.

Speaking to the doctor made me realise something I never thought was possible; I had postnatal depression. It made complete sense once the doctor spoke to me about it. I brought up Bryson and how I still missed him every single day, I just wanted him here too. Postnatal and grief all rolled into one is something I wouldn't wish upon my worst enemy. I was handed a script for anti-depressants, but as soon as I left the doctor surgery I ripped it up and threw it in the bin. Somehow, I still thought I was strong enough to handle whatever life threw at me, even though I had gotten myself into such a depressive state. I wasn't leaving the house, I stopped listening to music, which had been my saviour my whole life, I didn't even want to see Shelby. I couldn't allow her to see me so fucked up. The main two people who had to witness me at my worst were my children. Every time Lincoln would cry, I would cry and yell, *'Please just shut up for one second'*.

I never wanted to do anything with Hudson. He would beg to go to the park and I would say, *'Maybe tomorrow darling'*. One day I was a complete wreck. I just couldn't move from the lounge room floor; I would just lay with Lincoln as he cried and I would think, *'I'm better off disappearing'*. Hudson could clearly see I wasn't coping, he sat down next to me and said *'Mummy?'* I looked over at him, wiping away my tears.

'Yeah baby,' I replied.

Hudson went on to sing, *'Just keep swimming, just keep swimming'*.

My heart filled with so much joy, Hudson knew more than I realised. He watched my every move and if I went to my room to cry, he was right behind me cuddling me. I didn't want him taking on any of the responsibility of being there for me but he was a sympathetic kid who always made sure his mum was ok. *'Dad is at work, so I can help you Mummy,'* he would say. It just melted my heart.

Eventually, the time came for Ethel and Ron to meet Lincoln. They had tried to visit previously even though they had strict instructions to stay away, but Lachlan and I felt like the time was right for Lincoln to meet his grandma. The visit was nice, it was short but nice. Ethel held Lincoln until he spewed on her. Lachlan quickly grabbed Lincoln so Ethel could clean her jacket, and Ron refused to hold Lincoln. Apparently someone sneezed on him and he didn't want to spread any germs to Lincoln.

Once Ethel and Ron left, I was relieved. As much as they were lovely and there were no arguments, I still replayed every last thing that had been thrown at us from the pair of them since Bryson died. It just stuck in my head like glue. I could feel a storm brewing. Eventually I would snap, I just didn't know when.

It was only a few months since we moved to Adelaide when something really exciting happened. Lachlan was offered a posting to Cairns. We had only just settled in Adelaide but Cairns was somewhere we always wanted to live. We knew this opportunity wouldn't happen again. Lachlan and I said yes to the posting. We had five months left to enjoy Adelaide. I made sure to visit my sisters a little more often or they would visit me. Shelby would come over for dinner almost every night, I would visit her whenever I could. Ruth visited when she could. She was ready to have her twin boys any day now so we completely understood if she didn't want to drive her car or have visitors.

Things had gone a tad sour with Lachlan and Ethel. Lachlan never told me the full story because he knew I was already on edge but I think something was said about me so he stopped speaking to her. I ended up receiving an inbox from Ethel with a quote about how a son should treat his mother. The fury that ran through me was scary, I had that much anger I wanted to beat the shit out of this woman. I picked up my phone and called Ethel. The second she answered I abused her; it was like word vomit, I couldn't stop. Ethel hung up on me, so I called her back. I told her to come and meet me face to face because clearly our phone conversation wasn't getting us anywhere, which she agreed to.

Just after Lachlan finished work, I heard a knock on the door. I opened it and there stood Ron and Ethel. I think maybe Ron was there to intimidate me but at this stage I didn't care if she had an entire army with her, I was going to finally get out some built-up anger.

As soon as I started to speak Ron called me a bitch, and for the first time ever, I watched Lachlan stand up for me.

He walked over to Ron and said, *'Don't you dare talk to my wife like that, get out of my house now'.*

But I wanted Ron to stay to say his piece as well, which wasn't much. None of it made sense or was relevant to what my issue was with Ethel. Ethel sat in the corner very quietly, I would ask her a question and Ron would answer for her. I spoke about how we were treated in Adelaide for Bryson's funeral, how we were treated when Lincoln was born and why they didn't get why we were so over protective when it came to being vaccinated. Our words went unheard. Both Ethel and Ron just didn't care, and I was sick of trying to get it through to them about how important our son's life was to us. I ended up kicking Ron out, hoping that Ethel would stay and speak for herself or at least try to speak to Lachlan alone, but as soon as he left, Ethel got up to leave. I looked at her in disgust. She couldn't even stay to try and resolve anything. As she left in tears, I abused her and slammed the door shut. That was the last time I saw Ethel and Ron.

The night before we left Adelaide, we were meant to meet Ruth's twin boys but Ruth had been so busy with visitors, she forgot about us coming over. We were sad that we didn't get to meet them, but we knew how busy she was and there was always another time. Shelby and I said our farewells. Shelby asked that I didn't hug her goodbye or she would cry, so I gave her the finger instead. That was more her style anyway.

The next day at 5am, we drove out of Adelaide. Lachlan had asked if I would please listen to a song by Linkin Park.

'You know I hate music now, Lachlan,' I said.

But he insisted I listen, and I eventually agreed. Lachlan hit play and as soon as the music started the tears just fell from my eyes. The lyrics just spoke to me and reminded me so much of Bryson. The song was called 'One More Light'. I asked Lachlan to keep playing it over and over, it was the most beautifully written song that I had ever heard. As I listened to each and every lyric in the song, I knew that if Cairns didn't work out, and I was still grieving the way I was and disconnecting myself from my children, I was going to end my life.

A poem for Hudson

(I'm sorry)

I'm sorry I haven't been the same Mum that I used to be.

I'm sorry I haven't been there when you have really needed me.

I'm sorry you have seen me so sad and I couldn't tell you why.

I'm sorry you had to be the one to cuddle me, when I would cry.

I'm sorry I just shut off and ignore you some of the time.

I'm sorry Mummy has lost some of her sparkle and so much of her shine.

I'm sorry that you have had to suffer grief at such a young age.

Most of all, I'm sorry that Mummy is struggling with this chapter of her life and can't bring herself to turn the next page.

I love you Hudson.

Chapter 14

My healing space

Driving into Cairns was absolutely beautiful. It was so green, it felt like we belonged there. Our house was huge with a beautiful pool outside, which only made me panic about the boys drowning. Lachlan had already organised to go to Bunnings and get some bamboo to make the fence taller; he knew I would worry about it and was one step ahead of me.

As a family, we settled in really well in Cairns. I was so used to only unpacking half a house then storing the rest of our belongings but this time, Lachlan and I managed to unpack the entire house together. I came across an unopened envelope in one of our moving boxes. I opened it thinking it was something to do with Bryson, but it was the documents I received the day Lachlan and I left the hospital after I had a bleed very early on in my pregnancy with Lincoln. I read the letter. There were some really big words in there which I didn't understand, so I handed the letter to Lachlan to read. He was shaking his head as he read it. He picked up his phone and started googling the words I didn't understand, then showed me what they meant. I was in shock

'So I did have twins,' I said as my jaw hit the floor. *'I did have a fucking miscarriage.'*

We were both shocked, we didn't know why no one spoke to us about it on the day we were at the hospital. We didn't know how to feel either. We spent all this time not knowing we had twins, so we thought we didn't really have the right to grieve. Of course, we were sad and shocked but it had been so long since that letter was handed over to me, we just decided to try to see the positives in the situation and the fact we still had Lincoln here with us. I wish I could feel some positives when it came to Bryson, but I just didn't know where to begin.

As we were grabbing some stuff from the car, I picked up Bryson's urn, looked over at Lachlan and said, *'I think it's time we let him go'*.

Lachlan never went into a panic. He looked at me and said, *'Yep, it's time'*.

On Bryson's 2nd birthday, Lachlan, Hudson, Lincoln and I went to a beautiful waterfall. Lachlan climbed to the top with Bryson's ashes, whilst the rest of us waited below. At exactly 9:20am Lachlan released what we had left of our son. I was happy to see that Bryson was finally free of the urn, and he could fly high in the sky now. Lachlan climbed back down, grabbed me and cuddled me whilst the tears fell from his cheeks onto my t-shirt. I was so proud of Lachlan for doing what he did that day. It took strength and courage, something I felt I was lacking in at that stage, and I think maybe that was a little bit of a positive. I just didn't realise it at the time.

Hudson was almost four years old, which meant he could start kindy. We had looked around at some centres but nothing stood out to us, until we met Miss Tarleah from Bubblegum Day Care. This lady could make the saddest person on the planet smile. Tarleah just oozed happiness and her centre was great. I met the kindy teacher and the other children but it was Tarleah who had me sold! I booked Hudson in and he started kindy two days later.

It was only Lincoln and I at home during the day, which was really helpful for our bonding. I was still not really sure if I could completely put my whole heart and soul into loving Lincoln – I was still petrified of losing him. He had a monitor in his cot that would detect if he would stop breathing in his sleep just in case. I followed him everywhere around the house, and I even watched what toys he would chew on. I began to realise something as I was watching Lincoln out the back playing. If I didn't want to give my whole heart to my son, then why was I so protective over him? All this time I'd been worried about not loving him enough, when really, I was actually loving him just as much as I loved Hudson and Bryson.

From that day on, Lincoln and I grew closer. Lachlan would notice it; I would see him watching us playing and laughing together with the biggest grin on his face. I could feel my heart finally feeling that love I was too scared to feel, I would look at Lincoln and know he was my boy, and that was a massive achievement for me. I also noticed Lincoln was turning into a happier baby once I gave my all to him.

Although I was now bonding with Lincoln, my mental health was still a huge thing that needed sorting out. I needed a job or to study for my own sanity. I had to get some sort of normality back in my life. I decided to study early childhood education, it was something that would keep me focused for at least six months and if I decided I didn't like the course, I wouldn't follow through with looking for a job in childcare.

I went to my course three days a week, and although sometimes the classes were boring, I still enjoyed being around other people. I missed feeling normal for a day. One particular day, the other students and I were studying quietly when all of a sudden, the fire alarm went off. It was just a routine test, but I was instantly taken back to when I was having Bryson. The sound of the alarm was just like the heart monitor hooked up to me. I was shaking and fighting back the tears whilst other people sat at their chairs chit-chatting about the alarm being too loud.

As soon as the alarm stopped, I went home. I was so angry for allowing myself to be affected by a stupid fire alarm. As I paced through the kitchen trying to calm down, I looked over at a photo of Bryson hanging on the wall.

'This is your fault, you died and now I'm completely head fucked. Why did you choose me as your mum, if you were just going to die on me?'

These were the words I was shouting to a picture of my son on the wall. I fell onto the floor, crying and wishing Bryson never died. I wanted to hate him, so the pain would stop, but I couldn't hate him. In fact, I loved him so fucking much. I went through my bedroom looking for Bryson's hospital bag. I spotted it on top of a shelf in the wardrobe. I opened it up, and there it was, Bryson's newborn smell.

It was still in the hospital bag. I was going through the little outfits and nappies that were still neatly packed. I picked up his blanket and held it to my heart. The closest thing to a cuddle that I would ever get from Bryson again was from his blood-stained blanket. I slowly packed away his hospital bag and put it back on the shelf. Later that night I had made the decision to start running again. I was in a routine with studying, and I wanted to be the fit, healthy person I was in the past. Getting back into the groove of exercising was easier than I thought it would be; I would run on a trail that was filled with butterflies. I used to love seeing the bright blue ones fly past me, they reminded me of Bryson and I would smile as I kept running.

I never lasted long when it came to exercising, I would go for three or four days then hit rock bottom, then I would pick myself back up again, exercise another three or four days then slide back down that hill of grief. It was so fucking exhausting.

I was begging Lachlan to save me, I wanted him to save me from the pain in my soul. I just couldn't get through this on my own anymore. I tried to, I tried to prove how strong I was but I was destroying myself and my family by being too proud to seek help. I finally decided to go see a psychologist. I saw a few actually, and one of the psychologists said to me, *'How can we get you to start forgetting about Bryson?'* I left that session and never went back.

I ended up finding a beautiful lady by the name of Amy who specialised in grief. I thought Amy was definitely going to save me from my grief, my anger, my hate. I think I had three sessions with her when I realised something. Amy couldn't save me, Lachlan couldn't save me, absolutely no one could save me, except for me. I had to step up and start accepting my grief, accepting the new me. The me who cried all the time, and was now very sensitive. I also had to forgive myself for not only Bryson's death, but the hurt and pain that I had suffered throughout my life.

As soon as I came to terms with the fact that I had to just relax a little and accept that I had to grieve and to stop trying to just *"get over it"*, I was starting to forgive people who had hurt me throughout my life, and I hadn't even noticed I was forgiving these people. Carol randomly popped into my head one evening as I was trying to get to sleep and the hate I felt for her was gone. I still thought she let both Bryson and I down but I could think about Carol without wanting to beat the crap out of her. I knew I was very, very slowly starting to move forward which scared me. I didn't want to move forward and leave Bryson behind.

I ended up finishing my childcare course and was offered a job at Bubblegum, where Hudson and Lincoln both attended. I could start to see a speck of light at the end of the tunnel. I was actually feeling half human again, but Bryson's 3rd birthday was coming up and I was about to hit rock bottom hard and fast.

I started noticing a pattern with my grief. Every September I would start to grieve harder than normal, and by October I was depressed and not wanting to get out of bed. I would skip my psychologist appointments and just cry all the time. November would come around and I would be a complete fucking disaster. I would sit and think about Bryson all the time and if someone interrupted me mid-thought, I would totally flip out at them. I couldn't handle any sort of loud noises or too many people speaking at once. I would have to leave a room if there was too much going on, it just made me want to scream. By the time December 2nd arrived, I was fine. I still felt sadness, but I functioned better on Bryson's birthday than I did with the actual lead up. I still grieved after Bryson's birthday but it wasn't so intense.

I could see how much my roller coaster of emotions were affecting Lachlan. He had stood by for so long and watched me grieve; it was hard on him and I just wanted him to be happy. I would tell Lachlan to leave.

'Go and be happy,' I would beg. *'Please find someone who isn't like me.'*

Lachlan never left; he could have easily gone and never come back, but he didn't. He chose to stay and get through this torment together. As the months went by, I noticed a change in Lachlan. He started crying more about Bryson, not wanting to go to work or get out of bed. I asked what was wrong but I wouldn't get a proper answer from him. It suddenly hit me one day when Lachlan was laying on the couch – he was finally grieving Bryson's death. All this time he was worried about me and being the glue that held the family together. I was starting to have a somewhat normal life now which allowed Lachlan to step back and start to grieve. Lachlan started taking anti-depressants and seeing a psychologist straight away. I would hear him sleep talking at night, crying in his sleep, and he would sweat profusely. He was on struggle street that's for sure. I always spoke with him about his feelings and whether he was having a crappy day once he finished work.

I knew there was so much grief hidden inside of him which needed to come out. Lachlan had told me that he may be getting medically discharged from the Navy, which absolutely devastated him to even think about. We wouldn't know until later in the year, which made Lachlan's moods very low. We started to argue over the smallest, pettiest things; we just became sick of being in each other's face all the time. Neither of us knew what to do, and for once I was the one standing back feeling helpless. I didn't know how to make Lachlan better, except for allowing him to grieve however he felt necessary. Lachlan spent roughly three months in a really dark space, and just as I thought he was finally taking some steps to feeling better, he was told that he was definitely being medically discharged.

I had never seen Lachlan so disappointed in himself until the day he told me he was going to be out of the Defence Force. I tried my best to remind him that he makes his family proud every single day. If it wasn't for him, we would have nothing.

'I have no purpose now,' he said as he looked down to the ground.

I picked his head up, held his face in my hands and said, *'Look around you, your family are your purpose'*.

We didn't know where to move. I had loved my time in Cairns and I did more healing there than anywhere else, but it was time to go. We had discussed Darwin straight away, but I worried about schooling for Hudson and Lincoln. The only place we agreed to move was Adelaide. I liked the idea, I started to settle there last time so I figured it would be nice to start fresh there again. I just had to get the next few dark months to get out of the way before I could concentrate on finding a place in Adelaide.

September rolled around very quickly and I could feel the waves of grief crashing into my chest all over again and there wasn't a damn thing I could do about it. I would sit and think about Bryson all the time, replaying his birth like a movie inside my head, over and over. I would lay on the couch crying all day instead of going to work. I never slept, I would go to bed late and be awake at 4am thinking about Bryson and just as I would think that life wasn't worth living, the 2nd of December would come and I would be ok.

My healing space

Bryson's 4th birthday was here, and I decided that I would bake a cake for him and have the kids decorate it. Lachlan, Hudson, Lincoln and myself all sat at the kitchen table singing happy birthday to Bryson whilst four candles burned ever so brightly. I felt so sad but a little proud to see Hudson and Lincoln blowing out the candles on behalf of their brother.

The time had come to pack up and leave Cairns. Leaving Cairns was overwhelming as I had learned a lot about myself there; I also had some really dark times as well, but I would always be grateful for my time there. Cairns will forever be known as, 'my healing space'.

My darkest hour

I got out of bed today, although it was hard to do.

I went shopping and cleaned the house today and the whole time I was thinking of you.

I cuddled a photo of you today, with tears filling up my eyes.

I told people I was feeling ok today, knowing those words were all lies.

I played with your brothers today, wishing you were here playing as well.

Your big brother asked me where you were today, but that's a story I can't yet tell.

I went to bed tonight, wondering how I'm still alive.

How do I have a fucking pulse, when my heart went with you, the day you died.

Chapter 15

Your final chapter

We made it to Adelaide safe and sound. A friend of Lachlan's had offered us her unit to stay in until we could get our own place. We began looking for a rental straight away, somewhere near the beach was our ideal spot. I was still on struggle street with my anger and outbursts, it was eating me up. I could see my family suffering around me which made me try harder to be a happier mum and wife but I would only find myself becoming angrier the harder I tried. After years of trying to get through life the best I could, I caved and started to drink. The drinking numbed me, I enjoyed it. I would actually be happy, the kids loved seeing their mum happy but they didn't know it was alcohol-induced happiness.

The next day was never nice, I would wake up feeling like shit and moody as all hell.

I knew the path I was going down; I had been there before. After being absolutely wasted for six days in a row, Lachlan became concerned. He would remind me how bad I was in the past with alcohol. He didn't want to see me start something I wouldn't be able to stop and I felt the same way.

'I am going to see a doctor,' I promised Lachlan. *'I can't keep destroying my life and everyone else's around me.'*

It took a lot of courage for me to step into a doctor's office, tell my whole story and accept the fact that I had to take the anti-depressants I was prescribed instead of throwing the script in the bin. I wasn't going to take the pills and expect miracles to happen, that's not what it was about, I just needed some sort of balance inside of my head again. Lachlan clapped as I took my first anti-depressant. I don't think I've ever seen someone so proud of me for taking a drug before.

Over the next couple of weeks, I started to notice I was becoming a different person. I was feeling calmer, I wasn't snapping at the kids as much, I was starting to focus more on life and not so much about death. I can't say whether it was 100% the antidepressants or it was just me healing a little more, it could have been a mixture of both for all I know, but I was enjoying the feeling. Ruth had called to ask if we wanted to go to the beach, usually I would say *'No'* straight away or agree and change my mind last minute but this time I said *'Yes'* and actually went through with it. Hudson and Lincoln were very excited to play with their cousins, James and Patrick. As we got to the beach, the sun was shining, there were people swimming, walking their dogs, kids building sand castles. I couldn't believe I had been missing out on this sort of stuff for four years, and not only that, but my family missed out too. It was great seeing Hudson and Lincoln playing in the sand and hunting for seashells.

Ruth and I sat and talked about Bryson whilst Lachlan cooked lunch on his Weber, and a simple trip to the beach ended up being one of the best days I had in four years. I felt my heart flutter a little that day, I had this sense that Bryson was there right with me saying, *'Keep going Mum, I'm so proud of you'*. I walked down to the water, with Lincoln holding one hand and Hudson holding the other. I had tears running down my face as we put our feet in the water. Hudson and Lincoln played happily in the water, giggling as they splashed each other.

I smiled knowing that Bryson was right there with them. Although he couldn't be seen, I could just feel his presence. I closed my eyes for a minute and imagined Bryson being in the water too, looking at me with his beautiful blue eyes, giggling with his brothers and saying, *'Mum, come and play with us'*. I quickly opened my eyes as I felt a hand on my shoulder, it was Lachlan, he must have sensed I was having a moment.

'Is this all too much for you?' he asked.

I wiped the tears from my eyes and said, *'No way, I'm really enjoying today'*.

'I'm so proud of you Jasmin,' Lachlan said as he kissed my forehead.

I looked up at him and said, *'Thank you for never giving up on me'*.

We cuddled as we watched the boys making a sandcastle. It was a really special moment for me, one that I won't ever forget.

I had so many emotions running through me over the weeks, I really started to notice I was finally forgiving people. I had found out that Simone was having a baby which made me really happy, I ended up logging onto an old social media account that she hadn't managed to block me on and sent her a message. I went into the message knowing that I may not get a reply but I just had to tell her how sorry I was for being so distant from her when Bryson died, I didn't mean to push her away but I just didn't want her seeing me hurt so much. I was always the strong friend who would stand up for her if anyone upset her in any way. I explained my hurt when she cut me out, I congratulated her on being a mummy soon and I left the door wide open for her to respond.

I never got an answer from Simone, my message was read and was ignored. I had obviously hurt her in a way that she just couldn't forgive and my heart accepted the fact she never responded. I will always love Simone; she was a huge part of my life and I won't ever forget the beautiful friend she was. I had always hoped we would talk again but it was time to let her go now and move on with my life.

There was one person who I wasn't quite ready to forgive yet and that was Ethel. Ruth had asked if we wanted to have dinner with Ethel so she could apologise to us about the way she treated us when Bryson died. I thought long and hard about it. I was slowly forgiving everyone else but not Ethel. I had mentioned to Lachlan that I just didn't have it in my heart to speak to her yet, even if she did apologise. Lachlan took Hudson and Lincoln to see Ethel whilst I stayed at the unit. Lachlan called me on the way home and said that Ethel apologised to him for everything she had said and done since Bryson passed away. I was happy that Lachlan got an apology, he definitely needed one but I was just happy to hear how excited Ethel was to see Hudson and Lincoln. She never had to have a relationship with Hudson if she didn't want to but she never left him out. As much as she hurt me and made my life a nightmare at times, she was so good to her grandchildren. I don't know if I will ever mend my relationship with Ethel – time is a healer and I am still healing.

It had been two months since we had been in Adelaide and we couldn't find a rental anywhere. Lachlan and I were both becoming really frustrated. Lachlan suggested just packing up and travelling, neither of us had jobs yet or a house to call ours. As much as I wanted to travel, I just wanted to settle somewhere and send my kids to school and kindy when the time came. We all loved Queensland and the Gold Coast was my favourite place to visit but Darwin was still on my mind, I just kept having these urges to move back there. I never mentioned Darwin to Lachlan, I knew he wouldn't want to go back there so we decided on the Gold Coast. Ruth was absolutely devastated that we were leaving, we had only just gotten back and we were leaving again. I managed to squeeze in some time with my sisters before leaving, which was always great, especially when Shalanda and I would get together and talk about Jayme-Lee and Bryson. I loved talking to other women who had been through stillbirth, I didn't feel like an alien when I would talk about what I had been through.

I was desperate to see Shelby whilst I was in Adelaide but she had some personal issues happening that had kept her busy the entire time we were there. It sucked not saying goodbye to her but I understood why I couldn't.

Your final chapter

As we packed the car up for what felt like the 100th time, I just had a feeling we wouldn't be in Queensland long. I could hear Darwin calling our names and I knew it wouldn't stop until I spoke to Lachlan about it. After being in Queensland for two months and not feeling settled, I had to tell Lachlan how I was feeling.

'I just feel like I need to go back, I think it will help me heal,' I explained.

Lachlan looked me dead in the eyes and said, *'I have felt the same way, but I didn't think you would ever go back'*. We both knew Darwin was where we wanted to be, as much as we said we would never go back and we hated it there, we knew it was going to help us heal that little bit more.

I couldn't believe it. Here we were, packing up our car getting ready to move AGAIN!

I felt so bad for Hudson and Lincoln but they were great travellers and Hudson was excited to see his nana again. Although Mum and I never had much of a close relationship, Hudson and Lincoln loved her and she loved them. Mum's a hard one when it comes to forgiveness, I do forgive her for some things that happened when I was growing up but I will never understand why she didn't protect me from Rocco. Now that I'm a mum I know what it's like to be super protective and if someone ever hurt my child the way Rocco hurt me, I would happily do the jail time. It still hurts me to this day that I was the one who had to protect myself from a monster, no 11-year-old should have to go through that.

As we drove away from the Gold Coast I said, *'This is the last damn time we move,'* and I meant it.

On the way to Darwin I thought it would be nice to spend some time with Hudson's older brother, Liam. Gina, Liam's mother, and I had slowly become friends over the years. We would text and call each other to update each other on our boys. I thought it would be strange being friends with my ex-husbands first wife, but we didn't even see it that way. We spent four days with Gina and Liam. Gina had told me about her time with Tom and it killed me to listen to, it was all so familiar. I had thought about Tom over the years as I would grieve and I never hated him as much as I thought I would. I thought he would be one of the main people I would be so angry at but he just didn't affect me in that way. I was just as toxic for him as he was for me, although I never hurt him the way he hurt me. I always had some sort of appreciation for him, because he helped create Hudson and without all of the shit that came along with Tom, there would never have been Hudson and for that I am grateful.

Once we were back on the road to Darwin, we started to get excited. We hadn't been back since we drove away over four years ago. We stopped and had lunch on the grass in a tiny town right near the NT border. I looked around and saw beautiful flowers, birds singing in the trees and not a cloud in the sky. I appreciated nature a lot more since Bryson died, I appreciated the stars at night, I would always find the one shining the brightest and say, *'There's my boy'*. One of the biggest things I loved was when I saw a rainbow. I would happily stare at the colours, Hudson would always ask if Bryson was on the rainbow, Lincoln would get cross and say, *'No I'm a rainbow'* – he sure was our rainbow boy and I'm glad he recognised himself as one.

Our last stretch of the road was coming to an end. We were driving into Darwin, and I couldn't wipe the smile off my face. I had that instant feeling of *'We are finally home'*.

Lachlan was so happy to be back in the tropics again – it's where both of our hearts belonged.

Lachlan took my hand and said, *'Let's try this again, hey'*. I couldn't have agreed more.

Being back in Darwin has been the best decision for us. All four of us have suffered over the years – suffered way more than we should have. I have learned so much since Bryson left us.

Life, friends, hate, love, postnatal depression, seeking help and most of all, I have learned about forgiving and that sometimes it's a very slow process. I have been so hard on myself for so long, I hated myself more than I hated anyone else throughout my grieving journey. I am slowly learning to forgive myself for Bryson dying more and more each day. I have accepted that I can only take baby steps with moving forward. Grief is not a race, it's a slow, painful, bittersweet journey that I wouldn't wish upon anyone. I had a plan to finish this book with some amazing story that I was free from my grief, but September is almost here again and I'm the same mess that I have been every other year. I can feel the depression and anxiety building up, even as I write this. It's made me realise that a mother's grief for her child doesn't simply disappear, it stays in their soul for the rest of their lives, some months are good and some are really bad. The one thing I don't think I will ever be able to say *'Goodbye'* to is Bryson's hospital bag. It sits next to my bedside, where I am writing this last chapter of my book.

Something I was always afraid of when writing about my journey was leaving Bryson behind once the book was completed. It was one of my biggest fears, it took me so long to build up the courage to finalise every chapter, I just couldn't bear the thought of letting go of my son. I have only just realised, I can finish writing this book and have my baby Bryson move forward with me. I can't leave someone behind who is forever in my heart.

Bryson will always be with me until I die. When that day comes, I always imagine that when I I get to the big pearly gates, Bryson will be the one waiting for me on the other side, yelling out, *'That's my Mum and she's my hero!'* I will smile as the gates open and he runs into my arms. The hug I will get will be the one I have longed for, the one I could only ever think about for so long. Only this time, I won't ever have to let him go.

As you close the final chapter of my journey, please remember that my grieving chapter is never closed, it's forever open.

About the Author

Jasmin grew up in a little country town by the name of Port Lincoln in South Australia. She attended a local primary and high school. Jasmin has a love for music. She felt as though listening to songs with powerful lyrics helped her push through the hard times.

Jasmin made the decision to move to Darwin at the age of 22, where she met her now husband, Lachlan.

After moving around Australia with the Defence Force for a few years, Jasmin now lives back in Darwin with her husband, two beautiful boys and two dogs. Jasmin enjoys alternative therapies, and is a Reiki practitioner.

Jasmin enjoys spending quality time with her family, as she knows life is too short to sweat the small stuff, and has learnt to embrace the company of her loved ones.

CPSIA information can be obtained
at www.ICGtesting.com
Printed in the USA
BVHW081048211020
591502BV00001B/307

9 781922 497222